LEAD -ER- SHIP

No Regrets. No Retreats.

William Canary

Fulton Books
Meadville, PA

Published by Fulton Books 2022

ISBN 978-1-63860-709-0 (paperback)
ISBN 978-1-63860-710-6 (digital)
ISBN 978-1-63985-961-0 (hardcover)

Printed in the United States of America

To the loves of my life:
Leura, Will, and Margaret

No reserves. No retreats. No regrets.

—William Borden

CONTENTS

AUTHOR'S NOTE

*Everyone is entitled to his or her own opinion, but
they are not entitled to their own set of facts!*
—Andy Andrews

This book was written to help those in leadership, or seeking roles in leadership, hone the skills necessary to take charge. My aim is to simply offer a road map or to better reflect today's technology—a GPS route for those on a leadership journey. The best leaders are teachers who educate, instruct, motivate, and coach others. A leader teaches us to meet every moment with good humor, optimism, and kindness. A leader teaches us that a single person can turn challenges into realistic opportunities. A leader teaches us that one person can change the world. A leader inspires good people through mentoring and training. A leader also teaches the value of both forgiveness and compassion. A leader teaches the importance of telling the truth at all costs.

So why do I begin by suggesting that "prayer" has a quiet role in leadership? What are examples of prayer and leadership reinforcing each other? And what does it truly mean when a leader believes that prayer is so powerful that the blind can see and the deaf can hear it? Remember, you cannot move people to action as a leader unless you first move them with emotion. The head often follows the heart.

I offer these two examples for you to think about, reflect upon, and challenge yourself to apply it in your leadership journey.

The first example is comprised of the very first words spoken by President George H. W. Bush during his inaugural address on

January 20, 1989. In 1988, I was given the honor to head the first family operation at the inauguration on behalf of the then president-elect and Mrs. Bush. On that day, I stood in the very back of the platform terrace adjacent to the doors of the Capitol, through which every dignitary walked onto the swearing-in platform. It was a remarkable moment and something this "boy with a dream" from Long Island, New York, will always remember and treasure.

Following the oath of office, which was administered by Chief Justice William Rehnquist, and the twenty-one-gun salute that welcomes each new commander-in-chief, Bush spoke these heartfelt words:

> I have just repeated word for word the oath taken by George Washington two hundred years ago, and the Bible on which I placed my hand is the Bible on which he placed his. It is right that the memory of Washington be with us today, not only because this is our Bicentennial Inauguration, but because Washington remains the Father of our Country.
>
> And he would, I think, be gladdened by this day; for today is the concrete expression of a stunning fact: our continuity these two hundred years since our government began.
>
> We meet on democracy's front porch, a good place to talk as neighbors and as friends. For this is a day when our nation is made whole, when our differences, for a moment, are suspended.
>
> And my first act as President is a prayer. I ask you to bow your heads.
>
> *Heavenly Father, we bow our heads and thank You for Your love. Accept our thanks for the peace that yields this day and the shared faith that makes its continuance likely. Make us strong to do Your work, willing to heed and hear Your will, and write on our hearts these words: "Use power to help peo-*

ple." For we are given power not to advance our own purposes, nor to make a great show in the world, nor a name. There is but one just use of power, and it is to serve people. Help us to remember it, Lord. Amen. (President George H. W. Bush, January 20, 1989)

"There is but one just use of power, and it is to serve people"—words to be remembered by all in leadership. All leaders have a degree of power, and the just use is also to serve those you lead and your organization.

My second example occurred in the early morning hours of January 7, 2021, when Senate Chaplain Barry Black delivered a powerful prayer condemning the "desecration" of the Capitol building and reminding lawmakers of the weight of their words and actions just moments after Congress had affirmed president-elect Biden's electoral college victory.

Lord of our lives and sovereign of our beloved nation, we deplore the desecration of the United States Capitol Building, the shedding of innocent blood, the loss of life, and the quagmire of dysfunction that threaten our democracy. These tragedies have reminded us that words matter and that the power of life and death is in the tongue. We have been warned that eternal vigilance continues to be freedom's price. Lord, you have helped us remember that we need to see in each other a common humanity that reflects your image. You have strengthened our resolve to protect and defend the Constitution of the United States against all enemies domestic as well as foreign. Use us to bring healing and unity to our hurting and divided nation and world. Thank you for what you have blessed our lawmakers to accomplish in spite of threats to liberty. Bless and keep us. Drive far from us all wrong desires, incline our hearts to do your will and guide our feet on the path of peace. And God bless America. We pray in your sovereign name. Amen. (Barry Black, United States Senate Chaplain, January 7, 2021)

The words of both President Bush and Chaplain Black serve as a reminder that there is a saying in the ministry: "When God anoints, he enables." Maybe a better way to express those words is "If God brings you to it, he'll bring you through it."

But as you construct your own platforms for leadership, I can only hope that your determination to lead will allow you to draw upon many things in your life to give you strength to overcome fear as you head into a crisis that is going to happen.

President Bush and Chaplain Black understood the importance of change that required wisdom to inspire and lead. And in the pages that follow, I will share with you a case study of a real crisis of monumental consequences. It was my crisis to navigate my destiny.

As Warren Buffet said, "It takes twenty years to build a reputation and five minutes to ruin it." If you remember those words and, more importantly, live by them, you will lead differently!

INTRODUCTION

*If your actions inspire others to dream more, learn more,
do more, and become more, you are a leader.*
—John Quincy Adams

A Boy with a Dream—Leaders are Dreamers

When I turned sixteen, I came to this conclusion—I could be a leader. It was a near calling that happened while I was attending church services.

So you ask, you can be a leader based on what? Well, I realized in that moment that I could make decisions, which is the most important element in leadership. I had the passion, and I was willing to commit. Even at a young age, when I made a decision, I never looked back or gave it a second thought.

I also remember reading these words, or words to this effect, often attributed to John Wesley: "Light yourself on fire with passion, and people will come from miles around to watch you burn."

No one is going to follow you if they see indecision, hesitation, or a lack of courage to complete the mission.

Or was it from being a lover of music? Was this inspiration from the song "Get Up Stand Up"?

This iconic seventies reggae song was conceived while Bob Marley was touring Haiti and called for all to "Get Up Stand Up" and fight for greater equality in the world. Leadership is often about challenging the status quo, and sustaining yourself in such battles may require tremendous energy that can be difficult to sustain over time.

A leader who cannot passionately advocate for a mission will never attract and retain followers. Thus, wise leaders prudently take on the issues that give them the strongest sense of meaning and purpose. "Get Up Stand Up" captured and directed me to engage change with a passion.

So I decided to live life on the edge.

Or was it to come to me in the future from the words of Ferris Bueller? "Life moves pretty fast. If you don't stop and look around once in a while, you could miss it." Ferris organized people around a near-magical concept of leadership. He made it his mission to show others that the whole world in front of us is passing us by and that life can be pretty sweet if you wake up and embrace it. He had a vision.

As a sophomore in high school, I decided to run for student council president. In high school, we tend to identify successful leaders by three standards—grades, athletic accomplishments, and popularity. But I believed that a successful leader should be measured by defining the mission and simply accomplishing it.

I decided that in order to win, I needed to recruit a slate of candidates who could then encourage their friends to all support our ticket—an example of thinking ahead of the box. Despite being on this earth for less than six thousand days, I knew at age sixteen that I was lacking one critical skill set: experience. I was fearless, not reckless, and willing to fail by taking chances.

Or perhaps Pulitzer Prize-winning poet Mary Oliver spoke best about youthful leadership when she said, "As long as you're dancing, you can break the rules. Sometimes breaking the rules is just extending the rules. Sometimes there are no rules."

I decided I had the qualities to lead and asked myself, "Why not me?" At that time I was successfully juggling an expansive paper route, a neighborhood lawn-mowing business, and a frontline position at Burger King.

So when we won with a 95 percent turnout, I became president, and along with my newly elected slate, we began to change the world by taking command and control of our student government.

I became a leader who was first among equals of some 1,300 students. Immediately I labeled myself the CEO, but to me, the C meant to lead with clarity. E meant to lead by example, and O meant to lead with optimism.

But the election glow quickly evaporated as I began to learn that that being president of the student council required a keen understanding that there was a chain of command at St. John the Baptist High School. I reported directly to our principal, Father Mulligan, and our dean of students, Sister Bernadette Donovan.

I can assure you that they never bought into my theory that dissent based on principle was to be encouraged. I learned an important leadership lesson that being responsible sometimes means making people mad at you. If they were grading me on that, I would have received an A.

But that was not the case.

The first editorial ever written about me was published after my election in our school paper, *The Prophet*, and it said,

> *The Prophet* commends newly installed student council president Bill Canary for his demonstration of honesty. After only a few short weeks in his post, Bill has kept one of his most important campaigns promises—to establish contact between the student council and various extracurricular activities. As Bill pledged in his speech, the officers of the various clubs would be requested to report to the council on their various activities.
>
> *The Prophet* sees in this intelligent program two benefits: the much-needed contact between clubs and SC and the fulfillment of a promise upon which the president of SC was elected. Bill Canary is to be commended for his honesty and foresight. *This is sure to instigate the confidence of the student in its most important leader.*

I suppose I was simply a boy with a dream. This decision at the age of sixteen would lead me on a journey to destinations that I could have never imagined—first, as an elected official by twenty-five years of age, a member of a White House staff serving as the special assistant to the president, and a president and CEO of both a national trade association and a statewide equivalent of a chamber of commerce.

Not bad for a sixteen-year-old who simply believed he could lead others.

What are the lessons of leadership? What are the skills required to be a leader? How do you teach another to lead?

Frankly, I believe that leaders are making the life that they want for themselves. Born with the qualities to lead and applying their beliefs with an absolute conviction even in the path of resistance, leaders will always attract people they want around them because they convey both a sense of integrity and respect.

All leaders believe that you have to have both hopes and dreams, so part of the self-evaluation process is asking yourself, "Even though I've done great things so far, what's going to happen tomorrow?"

Think about this.

There are only seven musical notes. Only seven. Consider what Beethoven did with those seven notes.

There are only seven colors of the rainbow? Only seven. Consider what Michelangelo did with those seven colors.

Leaders can make the impossible look easy and develop themselves over time. You do not have to get everything right the first time. But when you make mistakes, learn from them, and realize there is no magic solution.

Leadership, in the end, is all about having energy, creating energy, showing energy, and spreading energy. "Get Up Stand Up." Leaders emote. They erupt. They flame; and they have boundless, and sometimes nutty, enthusiasm.

Just find your inner core and discern a clear vision and make it happen. Stated another way, leaders are dreamers who dream to change the world.

Your courage to lead must be greater than any fear of failure.

Leaders are held to a higher standard and are required to inspire others with both vision and courage.

In the end, I have been taught that leadership can be explained in six words—*No Reserves, No Retreats, No Regrets*—words that came from Christian missionary William Borden (1887–1913). He was a philanthropist and millionaire, and after finishing his Ivy League education, he boarded a ship for China to serve as a missionary. Due to his passion to reach the Muslim people, he stopped in Egypt to learn the Arabic language. While he was in Egypt, twenty-five-year-old Borden contracted spinal meningitis and within a month died. When Borden's parents were given his Bible after his death, they found the following written in it: ***No Reserve. No Retreat. No Regret.*** Powerful leadership lessons from a leader nearly 100 years ago. No reserve: Do NOT hold back. No retreat: Do NOT choose the easy path, go forward in what is leading you. No regret: Do NOT live cautiously. Lead to the fullest with this kind of spirit!

Those words are to me the true meaning of *carpe diem.* Make every day count—today, tomorrow, and the next.

Within these pages, you will not find a simple theory of how to lead, but you will find the waypoints necessary to set your GPS toward success as a leader.

We will explore baseline concepts on leadership.

We will learn that leaders have to have strong ideas.

Leaders are optimists and problem-solvers.

Leaders must display courage in the face of fear.

Leaders must embrace relentless preparation if they are to succeed.

But in the end, your willingness to take risks and responsibility will allow others to want to follow you. A leader learns that to get something you never had, you sometimes have to do something you never did.

A final thought—leadership is lonely. No matter how many members are on your team, often it is just you, and you alone.

Two places to seek guidance. First, look inside yourself for motivation and inspiration. And secondly, find inspiration from those leaders who have "been there, done that, and done it well." And it is okay to pray.

So let's begin this journey together.

CHAPTER 1

Make the Coffee — Collective Leadership

*The greatest leader is not necessarily the one
who does the greatest things. He is the one that
gets the people to do the greatest things.*

—Ronald Reagan

It is Monday morning, nearing 7:45 a.m., and you are first to arrive at the office. You turn on the lights, power up your massive Xerox copier, unlock the doors, and begin to ignite the coffee maker with inspiration. The team members arrive to the smell of coffee and the promise of a new day.

Do they wonder who made the coffee? Who advanced this simple moment of pleasure upon their behalf? Who can they thank? Who was this person?

Imagine their surprise to learn it was the person least likely to do so—the leader whose name appears at the top of the organizational chart. They appreciate what it means for a leader to make a meaningful contribution and, just as important, to do the right thing.

My favorite aspect of leadership is the people side of it. I love helping others to be successful.

When the people I lead are successful, I feel like I have been a successful leader. In so many ways, this is one of the most important reasons to lead.

So think about this. Do we need to display our titles? What does that mean in the world of leading?

Maybe another way to express this is to understand and believe that those you are leading can be viewed as business partners rather than mere employees. Empower them to make decisions, be responsible for others in the organization, and share in the success.

Let those you lead take turns leading. My goal was always to inspire others to feel like an equal. And while we had different roles and mutual respect in our respective roles, we shared our challenges and decisions as working together. Consider this: when you build your team, take into consideration sharing power and decision-making. Establish this relationship, and your team will always have your back.

In many ways, this can be described as collective leadership. What is collective leadership? Collective leadership for our purposes is a group of individuals in an organization who work together as a collective. They are encouraged to better understand the strengths, life experiences, intellectual capacities, and diversity of perspectives of the entire group and to further identify the capabilities of all its members to enhance making decisions and action-taking.

Making the coffee establishes an understanding that people come to work carrying baggage. That baggage can come in a variety of forms that challenge that person. They could be packed in as an illness in the family, marital tension, financial stress, extended family conflicts, or whatever it is, they carry it into the organization. No one comes to the work environment to do a lousy job. As leaders, we need to energize them, focus on their talents, and motivate them in the end, benefiting the organization.

When you adopt the principle that making the coffee is an extension of others seeing you as a leader, you establish a common set of values—that you lead by example, that you can take and you can give, that you hope to earn their trust and allow them to simply enjoy being around you, not as a threat but as a mentor.

General George Patton is a classic example of out-front-and-center leadership. His men loved and hated him—often in the same moment. They also knew he had the lowest casualty rates in every engagement because he was unafraid to commit his total resources. His men also knew that when he sent them into combat, he would go with them.

When critics said he endangered himself by leading from the front, he responded that he knew no way to lead from behind.

In my opinion, great leaders have always had the following strengths:

- Approachable
- Positive and Proactive
- Decisive
- Delegates
- Accountable
- Creates positive energy
- Does what they expect of others

You can't expect others to consider you a leader unless you have solid faith in your ideas. And once it's there, you build on it by being a good communicator, listening to others, setting examples, and not giving up. Remember that having the ability to show respect, empathy, and care to those that follow you are all attributed to being a strong leader while also showing that you care about their work or ideas.

The best leaders are committed to emerging leaders around them. They constantly work to create a strong team for accomplishing the mission. Leaders adapt to their surroundings and empower the team to succeed together. Leaders make the hard choice and self-sacrifice in order to enhance the lives of others around them. Push your team members to do, and be the best.

As a leader, understand that it's the people you lead that ultimately determine your success or failure. Having the ability to guide your team toward a well-defined vision by clearly communicating short- and long-term goals, inspiring confidence and trust. Leading others to want to serve a cause greater than themselves, leaders do not lead by forcing others to follow. Instead, a leader motivates.

They encourage others to follow them. They lead by example for others to follow. Leadership is never about who is in charge but a drive toward a coordinated goal.

And remember, leaders are rarely, if ever, satisfied with their performance.

You cannot please every person all the time. Just do the right thing and own it!

Can you now smell the coffee?

Chapter Review Questions

- How to grow leaders at all levels?
- How to increase employee retention from the top down?
- How to create better working relationships between coworkers across the organization?
- How to make your work environment more positive for your team?
- How to create positive and more productive teams?
- How to implement collective leadership as an exercise and training tool?

CHAPTER 2

No Titles on the Door — Just an Open-Door Policy

Leadership is not about titles, positions, or flow charts.
It is about one life influencing another.
—John C. Maxwell

True leadership doesn't require a title that comes with a corner office. What matters most—your title or your contribution to an organization?

Easy answer. Legendary management visionary Peter Drucker once said, "One does not manage people—the task is to lead people.

And the goal is to make productive the specific strengths and knowledge of every individual."

Leadership is about being authentic while diminishing drama at all levels.

Recognition is always the best path to overcoming drama and rewarding performance. Understand that "first among equals" needs to be displayed as being real and not simply a performance. Difficulty is inevitable. Drama is a choice.

In 2015, we undertook a massive renovation of our corporate offices. When the final touches to our new facilities were being completed, I was asked how we should apply the names and titles of our employees to their assigned offices. Should it be on a plaque next to their door or placed directly upon the frosted glass of each door?

At first, it seemed simple. Let's just do it the way we always did it.

But it struck me that it could be different.

You know I have often used the phrase "first among equals," and now it could be incorporated into our culture.

So we started with my door. Squarely in the middle of the frosted front portion of that door, the following words were assigned: William J. Canary.

Nothing more. Not my title, president and CEO. And zero references to my law degree, JD.

A foundational principle in leadership, much like the "no titles on the door," is having an understanding of what it takes to move a system. Fundamentally, the challenge is to cast your vision and have others want to join you in advancing that vision. Motives and objectives are what moves others, but leaders tend to give orders. Orders tend to simply deflate enthusiasm and erode a willingness to follow.

Rules for Picking Future Leaders

Look for intelligence and judgment and, most critically, the ability to anticipate. Also, look for loyalty, integrity, a high-energy drive, and the determination to get things done.

Making the Impossible Look Easy

During my time at BCA, I was fortunate to work with many talented individuals from various backgrounds, work histories, and life experiences.

However, there were three individuals who were truly exceptional, and I had the privilege of selecting and offering them an opportunity to become members of our team. In the cases of Mark Colson and Susan Carothers, it was their first job after graduating college. Nathan Lindsay had a tour of duty working for Governor Bob Riley as a personal assistant and, later, in his communications and policy shop.

Mark would work his way to the position as BCA's chief of staff, director of all political operations, head of governmental affairs, and interim president and CEO.

Susan would oversee our events and management affairs, which gave her responsibility for an annual fundraising dinner with more than one thousand guests and our annual summer governmental affairs conference, which hosted the legislature, the legislative leadership, the governor, the congressional delegation, our BCA leadership, and the business community of Alabama. In addition, she coordinated all activities with 124 chambers of commerce, serving as BCA's liaison for a period of time.

Nathan was the primary political operative at BCA. He oversaw our political action committee, Progress PAC, which raised more than one million dollars annually. In addition, he coordinated political strategy, polling, candidate selection, support, and logistics.

Three remarkable individuals that proved that picking the right people and mentoring them returns huge leadership dividends.

So some special ingredients for the magic sauce for *picking future leaders is an ability to anticipate. Also look for individuals with a sense of humor readily injected at those times when needed to make life manageable.*

Each one in his or her own right was able to not only grow into great leaders but also displayed a unique talent far beyond their respective ages, which *made the impossible look easy.* Collectively, they epitomized the word *professional* in every aspect of performance.

Their skill set was the *gold* standard in the Montgomery trade association world—leadership qualities that proved to be a testament to their ability to take BCA to the next level.

Further evidence of their leadership qualities included being conscientious, with an incredible capacity for constructive written work. They also possessed the ability to exercise good judgment, maturity, and ethical sensitivity to the entire staff and BCA organization. All three were results-oriented managers and proven consensus-builders who demonstrated concise strategic thinking skills.

As members of the senior staff, they were activists. Respectfully and consistently challenging the ideas of us all for the betterment of the organization is truly an important leadership quality that is essential to strengthening any organization.

In short, they always met and exceeded expectations. I was then, and remain today, very proud of them. Beyond friendship to me, they displayed unwavering loyalty to the organization.

Today, all three are thirty-something, and their futures have no limits. Working with them was a blessing.

Having an Open-Door Policy and Being a Teacher

To succeed as a leader, you must be willing to commit resources and energy and to encourage an open-door policy that will help inspire and retain great individuals. Staying behind a closed door will accomplish zero to advance your efforts to lead.

Open the door, share information, and invite others into the decision-making. You will be amazed how your team members will follow.

There are two words you must always remember: *motivate* and *educate.*

Leadership is the willingness to listen, and that applies especially when someone has something to say to advance the vision of the organization.

You want to create an atmosphere in which everyone feels they can approach and enter your office and speak their mind—totally unvarnished.

My core belief remains that everyone is entitled to their own opinions but not their own set of facts. If you bring a problem through that open door, you need to bring solutions along with it.

I wanted to create an environment that inspires people to make a difference and do a great job. Results are achieved by inspiring, not by barking orders.

A few weeks after all our names were placed on our doors, one highly respected team member, Dana Beyerle, was seen having his picture taken by his door. He was a seasoned and experienced individual who spent decades as a reporter for both local and national publications. A gifted writer and positive influencer to all in the organization, he was a member of the Tuscaloosa News reporting team that won the 2012 Pulitzer Prize for coverage of a tornado that killed fifty-three people, injured one thousand, and damaged or destroyed five thousand homes.

I asked him why he was having his picture made in front of his door. He told me that in all the positions he had ever held over a forty-year career span, his name never appeared on a door, and he was sending the photo to his wife. As a leader of an organization, you want to create an environment that produces energy, trust, initiative, and yes, even happiness.

Influencing lives and having individuals want to follow you is sometimes as simple as no titles on the doors.

Some final thoughts about the impact of no titles on the doors can be expressed as follows:

> Every single thing you do matters. You have been created as one of a kind. You may have been created in order to make a difference. You have within you the power to change the world. (Andy Andrews)

In *The Butterfly Effect: How Your Life Matters*, *New York Times* best-selling author Andy Andrews demonstrates how this amazing concept is illustrated in our own lives, and he makes the point that everything you do matters.

When Andy Andrews sent me his book, he inscribed these words:

To Billy,

This is a book about you! I am such a fan. Thanks for the difference you make every day in my life. Your influence and example are undeniable!

Your friend,
Andy

By making one move, you can affect a person's life.

I was invited to speak to the Student Government Association and a student leadership seminar with a selected group of honor students at Huntingdon College, a private Methodist liberal arts college in Montgomery, Alabama, by its president, J. Cameron West. President West, without a doubt, is one of the best academic leaders I have ever encountered. What he has built in nearly two decades is a direct result of his leadership, vision, and faith.

Huntingdon College today is truly a vibrant and thriving campus because of his courage and leadership.

I closed the lecture by reading a passage from Andy Andrews's book that detailed how Norman Borlaug and his one action changed history and may have saved two billion lives in the process.

A few days after my lecture, I received this handwritten note from a student leader that read,

Dear Mr. Canary,

It is always a delight when you come and speak. When you read *The Butterfly Effect* by

Andy Andrews to us, I thought it was a very enlightening story, and it gave me a different outlook on life. When I heard you were the speaker at our leadership lecture, I was overjoyed. The rules and concepts to become a better leader have already helped me tremendously. I have even passed on a few of those attributes of leadership to former teammates and other friends. As you know, being a leader is a serious job and nothing to take lightly. After hearing some of your nuggets of wisdom and experience, I know they will help me grow both as a person and also as a leader. Thank you for not only sharing your achievements but also the times of struggle and failure. I look forward to seeing how these leadership concepts help me not only now but also in the future. Once again, thank you for coming to speak with us.

Kindest regards,
Paige Taylor

PS: *Muscle Shoals* was indeed a great movie!

Always remember that your actions have value and can be a positive force in another's life.

Chapter Review Questions

- How to align leadership around the organizational purpose?
- How to engage team members in your purpose journey?
- How to anchor your strategy to the purpose of organizational leadership?

- How do you improve the skills of others by taking on additional projects and learn from other teams in the organization?
- Is there a butterfly in your life?
- What does "first among equals" mean to you?
- Do we need titles to lead?
- If yes, why? If no, why?

CHAPTER 3

The Diaper Story

Developing excellent communication skills is absolutely essential to effective leadership. The leader must be able to share knowledge and ideas to transmit a sense of urgency and enthusiasm to others. If a leader can't get a message across clearly and motivate others to act on it, then having a message doesn't even matter.
—Gilbert Amelio

A leader must focus on the future and set a vision for both the organization and the individuals that he will lead, but you need to figure out the best way to communicate this for ALL to understand.

A leader must also listen well. Listening is the key to effective communication. It is the one skill that creates the foundation for an effective communication platform.

- Leaders lead from the top down.
- Leaders fall forward.
- Leadership is a calling.

Great leaders are almost always great simplifiers who can cut through debate, argument, and doubt to offer a solution everybody can understand. The result will bring clarity of purpose, credibility of leadership, and integrity in terms that the members of the organization can readily understand.

This story was a favorite of mine and one that I used every time I was invited to speak to a group.

One evening, a very young professional baseball player and his wife found themselves home on a Saturday evening in the off-season, prepared to relax by watching a movie on Netflix.

The young couple were blessed with the birth of their very first child. The four-week-old daughter was put to bed, and they began to watch the movie. All of a sudden, they heard a scream and crying coming from their *daughter's* room.

Both raced to the room to check on her and discovered that the crying was the result of a wet diaper. The wife, wanting to return to the movie, asked her husband to change the diaper.

The young father, being very inexperienced and embarrassed (he did not know how to change the diaper), said, "What do you mean change the baby's diaper? That's not my line of work. I'm a professional baseball player!"

If looks could kill, this guy was in serious trouble. His wife looked him straight in his eyes and said, "LOOK HERE, BUSTER! THIS IS HOW YOU LEARN TO CHANGE YOUR DAUGHTER'S DIAPER. FIRST, YOU LAY THE DIAPER OUT LIKE A BASEBALL DIAMOND. YOU PUT SECOND BASE ON HOME PLATE. YOU PUT THE BABY'S BOTTOM ON THE PITCHER'S MOUND. HOOK UP FIRST AND THIRD, AND SLIDE HOME UNDERNEATH! AND IF IT STARTS TO RAIN, THE GAME AIN'T CALLED. YOU JUST START ALL OVER AGAIN!"

If she could find the common language to make him change his level of understanding, think what you can do.

Leadership is about creating an environment in which people want to be part of the organization and not just work for the organization. Leadership creates an environment that makes people *want to* rather than *have to*.

As a leader, I was obligated to create an environment that fostered feelings of investment, purpose, and involvement among all who worked with me.

It is purpose that leads people to truly give off their minds. Anything less is irresponsible to the organization and demands by handling individual team members.

When you see people only as pawns on a chessboard that fill a function, you are treating them like a thing—like the chair you are sitting upon. Instead, communicate with them clearly, often, and concisely, and use words and concepts they can embrace. Challenge others by giving them high standards.

And give them the tools, training, and unconditional support to pursue the goals and attain them.

The diaper story is a great illustration of how to put what appeared to be an impossible task into terms someone could readily understand and learn from. I love that story.

Communications is the oxygen for leadership.

During my tenure as president and CEO of the Business Council of Alabama, I would publish a monthly letter to a broad audience that included our officers, board members, and staff, as well as members of the state government's executive branch, the legislature, the congressional delegation, members of the business media, and our dues-paying BCA members, who we referred to as "investors."

The letter was generally three pages in length; and it explained the direction we were headed, our focus, our accomplishments, our challenges, and our clearly established vision as an organization.

Never miss an opportunity to communicate.

Always impart credit to many. Establish priorities to energize an organization, and yes, even discuss your failures.

In the end, you cannot wait for things to change because you must make change happen.

As a leader, how well do you see that change is a necessary agent to reach new levels, which embody communications skills to bring an understanding to all situations?

Gandhi said, "You must be the change you wish to see in the world."

The question will always be as a leader, will you change the world, or will the world change you?

Chapter Review Questions

- How do you communicate that taking pride in completing a task is a winning strategy?
- How do you communicate the importance of listening?
- How do you communicate that success reinforces good performance to motivate your team?
- How do you build rapport and synergy with your team to perform well?
- Can you communicate the complicated into the simple?
- What's your diaper story?

CHAPTER 4

Living on the Edge

Leadership Philosophy
If you're not living on the edge, you are taking up too much room.
—John Milne

Alan Alda said: "You have to leave the city of your comfort and go into the wilderness of your intuition. You cannot get there by bus, train, or car, only by passion and a sense of adventure. Not quite knowing what you are doing, what you discover will be wonderful. What you discover will be yourself. What you discover will be how to lead."

Experienced leaders know instinctively that procrastination in the name of reducing risk is an increased risk. People with all types of personality traits and a wide variety of temperaments have become effective leaders. If that is the case, it is useful to determine the common traits that long-term leaders generally possess.

Characteristics:

- Empowering (using more of your heart than your head)
- Credible (trusted)
- Visible (far out front)
- Decisive (making appropriate and timely decision)
- Calculate the risks but take them (failure not an option)
- Believe in yourself (confidence)
- Have no regrets (never look back)
- Self-control (discipline)
- Be bold (courage)

So talk about leaving the city of your comfort and go into the wilderness of your intuition.

In late 1994, our family moved from Washington, DC, to Montgomery, Alabama. My wife, Leura, (born and raised in Alabama) was working as a lawyer in the civil division of the US Justice Department at the time, and she was offered a job allowing her to head the same division in the US Attorney's office of the Middle District of Alabama. The decision to accept that post would later result in President George W. Bush appointing her as the U.S. Attorney for the Middle District of Alabama in 2001. This appointment would make her the first women nominated by a President to serve as a U.S. Attorney in Alabama's history.

The decision to move was in the best interest of our one-year-old son Will because it brought us geographically closer to Leura's family, and it also allowed me to start a consulting practice and test my abilities in the hand-to-hand combat of politics learning now, to navigate on both sides of the political aisle. One individual I was introduced to was John Anzalone (from Michigan, now living in Montgomery, Alabama) who would become one of the premier democratic pollsters in America by the 2020 election cycle. He remains a wonderful friend twenty-five years later and our political differences have served to make us better people and leaders.

In 1998, I was introduced to Mike Hubbard, a thirty-six-year-old from Auburn who wanted to run for the Alabama House of Representatives. That introduction was advanced by the brother-in-law of freshman congressman Robert Aderholt, who had recently been elected to represent a largely rural district in North Alabama.

Just thirty years old at the time of his election, Aderholt was the youngest person to be elected to Congress in the 1996 cycle. I served as the general political consultant (joined by two brilliant political operatives Brian Rell as campaign manager and Jim McLaughlin for polling) for his congressional election, which he won by less than 1 percent of the vote, and twenty-five years later, we all remain close friends. I still proclaim that his wife, Caroline, had the most natural political instincts of anyone I had ever known, and she remains an amazing visionary today.

After our meeting, I agreed to serve as Hubbard's consultant on his campaign for the legislature. Initial polls showed us with a nineteen-point deficit in June, but we pulled off a political miracle and won by a sixteen-point margin in November.

Within a few years, State Representative Hubbard decided it was time to elect a pro-business conservative majority in both houses of the legislature, even though Democrats beholden to labor unions had held control for each of the past 136 years. Working in tandem with then-governor Bob Riley, who was just the third Republican to hold that office since Reconstruction, a strategic plan that included fundraising, messaging, and grassroots-organizing was created and put in place.

Hubbard was the architect of the plan that resulted in a political tsunami on Election Day in 2010. His vision, leadership, and self-sacrifice, coupled with determination and relentless hard work, won conservative supermajorities in both chambers and changed politics in Alabama forever. His colleagues rewarded him with election as the first Republican Speaker of the House in more than a century.

The self-confidence, blind faith, and willingness to throw caution to the wind that Hubbard displayed inspired many across the state to follow his leadership, even though there was a steep political price to pay if the mission of capturing the legislature had succeeded.

In all fairness and transparency, I should disclose at this point that Mike is my brother from another mother, my best friend, and one of the best strategists with whom I have ever shared a political foxhole. His wife, Susan, is a brilliant and talented educator, and he and his family are considered members of our family.

One of my favorite generals from World War II is General Anthony McAuliffe. During the Battle of the Bulge, the Allies were struggling against a large Axis force, and McAuliffe called his leadership together. He told them in no uncertain terms that they were surrounded by the enemy, but in the next breath, he noted they were faced with one of the greatest opportunities ever presented to an army. They could attack in any direction.

His example is the epitome of optimism and living on the edge!

In 2001, I had the privilege to lead the American Trucking Associations, and I was serving as the president and CEO on September 11. Like millions of others, we watched on television as the first and second planes struck the World Trade Center towers. From my eighth-floor office, I could see Reagan National Airport and the Pentagon, which were located just a few miles away.

At around 9:39 a.m., after the Twin Towers had been hit but before they collapsed, a 757 that had been captured by terrorists approached the Pentagon. Having flown over the capital city from the north, it ultimately made a 270-degree turn before deliberately crashing into the Pentagon, killing all 59 who were onboard and Steve Brooks my chief of staff was by my side that entire day and evening. Steve was my friend and prayer partner dating back to our days together at the Republican National Committee in 1992. With Bible in hand, we visited with every member of our staff individually and offered them comfort, prayers and hope.

A wonderful person and valued friend of mine, Barbara Olsen, was among those who were on American Airlines flight 77. A legal analyst and television news commentator, she had worked at the US Justice Department, served as a congressional investigator, and was a general counsel in the Senate.

Barbara also authored the book *Hell to Pay*, and in the copy she gifted me, she wrote,

December 10, 1999

To Billy Canary,

I hope they find your FBI file—or at least identify whose fingerprints are on it!

All the best,
Barbara Olson

Barbara's mention of "finding my FBI file" was a direct reference to the controversy that arose when the Clinton administration was caught improperly accessing the FBI security-clearance documents of Republican political operatives and former White House officials. Craig Livingstone, director of the White House Office of Personnel Security under Clinton, had requested and received from the FBI the background reports of three hundred individuals without seeking appropriate clearance.

My file was among the three hundred.

Allegations were made that senior White House figures, including First Lady Hillary Rodham Clinton, may have requested and read the files for political purposes. The matter was investigated by the House Government Reform and Oversight Committee, the Senate Judiciary Committee, and the Whitewater Independent Counsel. In 1998, Independent Counsel Kenneth Starr exonerated President Bill Clinton as well as the first lady of any involvement in the matter.

Barbara served as an inspiration to so many of us by her courage, integrity, and fearless desire to seek the truth. Our world was a better place because of her, and after 9/11, a huge hole existed in all our hearts and lives.

The plane crashed into the Pentagon's facade and exploded, swallowing the massive building in a cloud of smoke and leaving a gaping fiery wound in its side. The explosion was felt in our headquarters office, where we could easily see the fireball that resulted. All of us understood that America was under attack, and I knew at that moment that the trucking industry would play a major role in the days to come.

By presidential order, all flights were cancelled and grounded. All trains came to a halt. Buses were parked, and ports were closed. But the trucking industry continued moving along and provided assistance wherever needed. I would coin the phrase "On duty for America 24/7/365," and as the article below suggests, I made it a central theme in my keynote speech to the two thousand assembled attendees at our annual industry meeting in Florida just one year later.

Canary Offers No Apologies for Industry

American Trucking Associations' president William J. Canary told attendees at the Management Conference and Exhibition that he has been honored to serve "an industry that I love, an industry I will not apologize for."

In his comments, Canary painted trucking as an unheralded but vital industry.

"Think about the vitality of this industry, bringing the Halloween candy that fills the grocery store aisles, the costumes, in the end bringing most of what our families consume," Canary said. "And yet again, when you think about it, all of this is done without the fanfare that it deserves. It's almost magic—it just happens as if there isn't a father or a mother, a brother or sister out on the roads doing their job so that we can do ours."

In highlighting ATA's achievements in the past year, Canary talked about his mission to strengthen the bond between state associations and their members and ATA.

Canary told convention goers that "trucking is a simple industry with a simple mission—to deliver goods safely, to turn a profit, and to provide a living for the millions of people that rely on us each and every day."

Touting trucking's contributions to the economy, Canary emphasized that the industry has nothing to apologize for.

"The truth is that more people should be thanking us because without trucking, America stops, and that is something that we will never allow to happen on our watch," Canary said.

Canary also pointed to trucking's contribution to the War on Terrorism in the thirteen months since the September 11, 2001, terrorist attacks.

"Never has 'On duty for America' been more appropriate than this very week. Last year, I stood here and told you how we witnessed a tragedy, a senseless taking of life that affected each of us. This year, while not of the same magnitude for many, I also stand before you are following a senseless tragedy," Canary said. "Using our Highway Watch program, which trains drivers to be vigilant on the roads that they drive, we issued bulletins from the police that they felt would be helpful in apprehending the villains responsible for the killings."

Canary's address was the highlight of Monday's general session of the Management Conference and Exhibition in Orlando, Florida.

I have always believed that the best leaders lead by who they are and what they do. During my tenure at the American Trucking Associations, serving as its president and CEO certainly were not days of comfort and ease but rather days of challenge and fear. Every great leader I observed over the years was a person running away from things but also running toward things. I learned that fear in my case was a wonderful motivator.

When I fell forward to accept the president and CEO of the Business Council of Alabama, this editorial will always remain as a source of pride in my leadership journey at the American Trucking Associations.

Editorial—Passing the Baton

Transport Topics
January 16, 2003

The responsibility for leading American Trucking Associations passed this week from William J. Canary to Bill Graves. ATA was transferred from one professional and competent set of hands to another.

Canary assumed the helm of the nation's leading trucking trade group as interim president in July 2001 and later agreed to become the official, but temporary, president until Graves finished his second term as governor of Kansas.

Now that he has turned over his state office to his successor, Graves is scheduled to officially assume the presidency of ATA on January 15.

Canary's tenure will surely be best remembered for his building of bridges between the national organization and its state affiliates and councils. It was his top priority.

His success in that arena should come as no surprise since Canary had overseen federation relations for ATA for several years from his home in Alabama before taking on the presidency. He is a leader committed to compromise and consensus.

During his tenure, he helped restore a full measure of trust, which had frayed under the pressures of ATA's restructuring, between the national federation, its councils, and state trucking associations.

The bonds between ATA and the Truckload Carriers Association and the National Automobile Transporters Association were rebuilt. And there are ongoing discussions with other groups over efforts to form a coalition that can speak for all of trucking.

Despite economic hard times, ATA has grown in strength and influence.

The federation ended 2002 with more members than it had at the beginning of the year, the first time that's happened in a long time. It's one of the measurable outcomes of Canary's stewardship.

As a result, Graves will inherit a stronger and more powerful ATA.

With this solid platform, Graves can be expected to move ATA to new levels of influence, thanks to the reputation he built during his eight years as the political leader of Kansas. Graves comes from a trucking family and is already familiar with many of the major issues facing the industry on Capitol Hill, at the White House, and with the federal regulatory agencies.

ATA is indeed fortunate to have this kind of strong leadership. This is a time to thank Bill Canary and to welcome Bill Graves.

Leading a national trade organization is a rare privilege; and every day I tried to use my character, integrity, and faith to inspire others as a servant leader. And the quote at the head of this chapter became a daily reminder of where I found myself in these times of challenge. If your true worth is to be assessed using your character as a yardstick, where do you stand? Who is going to measure it? How? By what standard? Your true character comes out in its starkness, frankness, and fullness when you are on the edge.

"If you're not living on the edge, you are taking up too much *room.*"

Chapter Review Questions

- Have you passed a baton?
- What were the circumstances?
- Is it fair to say that winners take more risks than others?
- How do you stay positive and calm in challenging times?
- How do you create a feeling of optimism and hope in the face of fear?
- Are you living on the edge or simply taking up room in your leadership journey?

CHAPTER 5

50/50 Rule—Leading with Yes

Do or do not, there is no try!
—Yoda, *The Empire Strikes Back*

So what are the chances of making a wrong decision?

What percentage would you apply?

Might it be 10, 20, or even 30 percent? Or might it simply be just 50/50? As Yoda explained to the young warrior, "Do or do not, there is no try."

Leadership demands that you can make decisions.

An important principle of leadership is that leaders are people of action, and people of action will create opportunity. You will move obstacles out of the way and inspire people to follow your lead. If you elect to ignore taking action, you will not be free from the consequences of staying in place.

Yes vs. No

- For many, saying *no* is safe.
- *No* goals, *no* direction, *no* ambition, *no* vision, and *no* plan. As a rule, *no* doesn't lead us forward.
- Instead, say "Yes!" because *yes* is courage.
- *Yes* leads with goals and a plan. It is not always easy to say *yes*.
- *Yes* means taking chances, being courageous, putting oneself out there, and embracing the future.

Leaders understand these simple lessons in 50/50 rulemaking— leading with yes and being "good tired" (which I will explain shortly):

- Be credible, trustworthy, and honest.
- Be positive with perpetual optimism.
- Stay committed.
- Embrace the power of information.
- Encourage dissent based on principle.
- Always act in a professional manner.
- Show respect.
- Never give up.
- Have fun in your role.
- Inspire others.
- Do your homework.

One great fiction about leadership is that everyone will immediately align with a leader's mission, goal, and vision. It is noted that the leaders who are often seen as great leaders welcome dissent based on well-informed principles. This is an important component of empowering those you lead. Your job is to ensure those who follow you that it is acceptable and safe to express dissent. Encourage them to pick a side and voice an opinion.

Being responsible sometimes means making people mad at you. Leadership involves responsibility to the welfare of the group, which means that some people will get upset at your actions and decisions.

Trying to get everyone to like you is a sign of mediocrity, and you will avoid the tough decisions.

Trust a leader who shows up, makes the tough calls, takes the heat, sleeps well amid the furor, and then aggressively chomps into the next task in the morning with visible vitality.

Good Tired vs. Bad Tired

Harry Chapin was a storytelling singer-songwriter who died far too young. I had the privilege to know him as a fellow Long Islander and became a huge fan of his music after first hearing him perform on my college campus.

This story is about his grandfather and the importance of training yourself to always chase your dreams and fight hard rather than focusing solely on winning.

> My grandfather was a painter. He died at age eighty-eight, he illustrated Robert Frost's first two books of poetry, and he was looking at me and he said, "Harry, there's two kinds of tired. There's good tired and there's bad tired." He said, "Ironically enough, bad tired can be a day that you won. But you won other people's battles; you lived other people's days, other people's agendas, other people's dreams. And when it's all over, there was very little you in there. And when you hit the hay at night, somehow you toss and turn; you don't settle easy.
>
> It's that good tired, ironically enough, can be a day that you lost, but you don't even have to tell yourself because you knew you fought your battles, you chased your dreams, you lived your days and when you hit the hay at night, you settle easy, you sleep the sleep of the just and you say, 'take me away.'

He said, "Harry, all my life I wanted to be a painter and I painted; God, I would have loved to have been more successful, but I painted, and I painted and I'm good tired and they can take me away."

This story is beautiful, poignant, and inspirational all at once. The wins and other such results hardly ever matter.

When you lead as a yes leader, well, that is being "good tired."

What if all those whose opinions you respect tell you *no*?

What if all in the dissent tell you *no*?

If you believe in something that has never been done but everyone tells you it will not work and works against you, do you still go forward? The simple answer is *yes*. To me, it speaks of the power of the struggle for a cause that we feel strongly about. The wins and other such results hardly ever matter.

That is exactly what I did during my first year as the leader of the Business Council of Alabama, and it made me "good tired."

The Partnership and the Business Education Alliance

I want to share with you two examples to illustrate the ability to lead in waves of *no*. In both these initiatives, *doing* was the only option.

The First Initiative—Partnership Leverages: Strengths of State and Local Chamber Business Advocates

By way of background, since its beginning in 1937 as the Alabama Association of Commercial Organizations, what would become the Chamber of Commerce Association of Alabama remains dedicated to advancing the goal that chambers of commerce are the premier local business advocates in the state of Alabama. In conjunction with the Business Council of Alabama, the two groups, through the CCAA/BCA partnership, represents the interests and concerns of more than one million working Alabamians.

Now, I will tell you the story of why I decided to do what many claimed was the impossible. Those in the "no" column believed these two organizations could not be united. Others had tried, and all failed. What was different now?

Maybe it was the fun of proving the naysayers wrong. Maybe it was the desire to feel "good tired" and to do the right thing.

In 2003, the leadership of the Business Council of Alabama (BCA) and the Chamber of Commerce of Alabama (CCAA) formally inked a historic agreement that leveraged the five-thousand-member companies of the BCA with the more than 120 local chamber executives comprising CCAA and the nearly sixty-thousand-member businesses they represent.

The partnership would take on a life of its own, strengthening grassroots understanding and support for key issues vital to Alabama's business climate and economic growth and providing an efficient mechanism for mobilizing business leaders throughout the state.

Former CCAA chairman Rick Roden, president and chief executive officer of the Greater Jackson County Chamber of Commerce, got right to the point when asked about his opinion of the program. "The partnership has created grassroots potential like never before seen in the state of Alabama," he said.

Going forward on the strength of the partnership, BCA was not just communicating with five thousand businesses and industries, we were reaching out to nearly sixty thousand. Through the local chamber network, we had an even broader view of the challenges facing Alabama businesses ranging from the largest employers to small mom-and-pop operations and a precision mechanism for addressing those challenges efficiently and effectively.

A Model Program

Former CCAA president and CEO Ralph Stacy said, "The partnership is the first of its kind in the United States and already has become a model for other states hoping to connect and mobilize their business communities."

The US Chamber of Commerce was also intrigued at the thought of the grassroots potential that would be unleashed if partnerships like ours were developed between state and local business groups across the country. The American Chamber of Commerce Executives has asked us to spearhead a national platform to identify how Alabama's partnership can be used as a template for other states.

While the partnership birthed the natural liaison between the like-minded state and local business advocacy organizations, its success is likely due to the fact that each group remains autonomous and neither is bound by positions taken or programs advocated by the other.

"The partnership gives local chambers of commerce a presence at the state and federal levels never before seen by most chambers," said John Seymour, president and CEO of the Decatur Morgan County Chamber of Commerce and CCAA chairman when the partnership was launched. "Yet while forging a strong bond to build a better Alabama, both groups retain their own unique identities."

That concept remains in full swing today some seventeen years later as CCAA members across the state connect with BCA governmental affairs professionals for routine "legislative update" conference calls when Alabama's legislators are in session. The conversation addresses legislative proposals that stand to affect business bottom lines or economic development. The local chamber executives and their volunteer leaders, who are also invited to participate, commonly want insight into the actions or votes of their local legislators.

Knowledge is power, and the sharing of information remains an absolute win-win for both the BCA and the local chambers. Communication was the lifeline of the partnership, and the conference call—and Zoom-type updates gave local business leaders keen insider perspective into the actions of their lawmakers so they could thank them when they support important pro-business initiatives or voice their displeasure when they did not. When it comes to getting a lawmaker's attention, the folks back home always carry the biggest stick. As Tip O'Neill is often credited with saying, "All politics is local."

In addition to the coordinated mobilization of state and local resources when it comes to policy issues, the partnership has proven an effective tool for rapid-fire communication and action during crisis, an originally unplanned but especially positive result of the union.

The first test came during the devastating aftermath of Hurricane Katrina. BCA and CCAA joined forces to gather and transmit information about businesses, individuals, and recovery resources available to assist companies victimized by the destruction.

The BCA/CCAA Recovery Assistance Clearinghouse came together quickly as BCA's expertise and reach into state and local government were critical to the gathering of valuable resource information and CCAA's ready-made network into the local chamber community meant the essential details got into the hands that needed help the most. The Hurricane Help Center was an example of the partnership at its best. Timely information, combined with targeted distribution, helped get resources where they were needed. That meant businesses in storm-ravaged areas could reopen sooner and put people back to work sooner.

This partnership approach to crisis communication caught the attention of the US Chamber's Center for Corporate Citizenship, which added the BCA/CCAA partnership to its nationwide network dedicated to marshaling support for hurricane victims. As a result, offers of help for Alabama businesses came from as far away as Michigan, Iowa, and California.

The United States Chamber of Commerce said, "We owe somebody in Alabama a royalty for creating such a model program."

It is incredibly gratifying to have been proactive with an idea that is recognized as visionary by many outside the borders of Alabama. We made a real difference in Alabama, and watching the ripple effect it has caused across the fifty states has been exciting.

Like any enterprise, its success has been predicated on teamwork—no egos and no personal agendas, just dedicated business advocates intent on leveraging their individual strengths for the greatest impact. CCAA gains from its relationship to BCA's large membership and strength at the state level. BCA gains by having access to the thousands of businesses that are members of their local chamber of commerce. In the end, the result was a unified and coordinated effort at the state and local level and a winning team for Alabama business leadership.

The Second Initiative—Business Education Alliance (BEA)

Why did I invent the Business Education Alliance? Simple. The business community in Alabama was, by far, the largest consumer of the product created by our state's school systems, so it is imperative that graduates possess the skills and education that the twenty-first-century workplace demands—period.

But the recipe that made this work was found in two individuals: Joe Morton and Jay Love. Morton, the chairman of the BEA, is an educator with four decades of experience who served for seven years as Alabama's state superintendent of education.

Love is a small businessman and former legislator who chaired the House Education Ways and Means budget-writing committee and currently serves as the finance chairman of BEA.

They took the impossible and made it happen. They believed in it and were committed to succeed as long as I would provide my unqualified support as the leader of the Business Council of Alabama.

I told them to take *yes* for an answer!

During their parallel careers as an educator in one case and as a legislator in the other, it was not uncommon for them to see special interests in Alabama working to pit the business community and the education community against each other in order to promote selfish agendas or to pursue flawed political goals. They had the background, experience, integrity, and passion to lead the BEA. Communicating was the second ingredient in the recipe of success.

In 2013, the Business Education Alliance mission was to unite two groups that will determine Alabama's economic future—the educators who produce the members of tomorrow's workforce and the business leaders who will one day employ them.

BEA was created to stimulate the thoughtful study and constructive discussion of key policy issues facing Alabama. Our goal was to jumpstart solutions to the problems that we faced by promoting interactions between the public and private sectors.

We believed that combining the workforce needs of business with the best and most innovative ideas in public education would result in Alabama becoming a national leader in both economic development and student achievement.

BEA brought like-minded people from the business and education communities together to boldly forge a new direction for our state and to sometimes simply remain committed to a plan that yields the results we want and need, even though they it might not materialize overnight.

In America's highly political atmosphere, it is refreshing to see a group that is dedicated to bringing interests together rather than driving them apart.

The business community has long been an advocate for the professional teacher and has a strong record of support for quality classroom initiatives for our children.

It was our obligation to work with those in the education community to provide to Alabama students an opportunity to receive a first-class education.

Anything less was unacceptable.

Participating in the politics of division is a sport in Alabama, but our students are the ones who suffer when these tactics are used to divide those who care about improving education.

Today's students are tomorrow's workforce, which is why I had, for years, been advocating for such an alliance between business and education.

To compete and lead in today's global economy, Alabama must be a global leader in education.

The answers to solving this problem are best suited to come from the local and state level, which is why I created the Business

Education Alliance to ensure that twenty-first-century jobs are filled with individuals that have twenty-first-century skills.

Improving our public education system is not about partisan politics or any hidden agenda.

It was simply about providing each Alabama student what is deserved—an opportunity to get a quality education, which lay a foundation for future success.

Perhaps no group depends upon the product of our public education system more than Alabama's businesses and industries. Rather than working to divide business and education by promoting fear and waging campaigns of misinformation, the Business Education Alliance vision was to unite the two so that students and parents are better served, our economy is improved, and Alabama employers are guaranteed the trained and effective workforce they need in order to remain here.

Our message was simple: *Alabama cannot succeed economically without also succeeding in the classroom.*

During the past decade, Alabama has experienced encouraging results in public education and job creation, but those results have not been consistent or uniform across the state.

Moon landings and the International Space Station have their roots in Alabama, and commercial airplanes are now made here. A variety of automobile manufacturers and suppliers employ thousands upon thousands of Alabamians at highly attractive wages, and our medical and biotech firms are making life-changing breakthroughs.

And rather than seeking to divide and separate interests, BEA was to be both pro-business and pro-education because in the end, both communities have a shared goal—propelling Alabama into a position of national and international leadership in economic development and education excellence.

Don't be afraid to speak out.

Don't be afraid to be a yes person.

Collaborate, communicate, and publish that which needs to be heard. In the end, your impact will surprise you.

One such example:

Choosing Alabama's next state superintendent
William J. Canary and Joe Morton
Alabama Voices
Montgomery Advertiser
July 15, 2016

Whether it's becoming a doctor, teacher, lawyer, pipe fitter, welder, or automobile assembler, education is the key to filling tomorrow's jobs.
Anatoliy Babiy/Getty Images/iStockphoto

We support the State Board of Education in its duty to select our next state superintendent of education and firmly believe it is the decision of the nine-member board to select the best person from those who have submitted applications.

While in no way are we trying to influence the vote or the final selection, we do believe that any select group of candidates interviewed for the job should be asked in a public forum a group of questions that will give insight into how a new state superintendent of education will lead public education in the years to come.

The following list of pertinent questions is essential so the public, those in the education community, members of state government, the legislature, and the business community can be informed about the candidates:

- The Alabama Reading Initiative (ARI) was created to enable every student in Alabama public schools to read, at a minimum, at grade level by the end of the third grade. In 2011, Alabama achieved a milestone in reading by seeing its fourth-grade students score at the National Average on the National Assessment of Educational Progress (NAEP). Since then, the NAEP fourth-grade scores in Alabama have declined. As state superintendent of education, what will you do to revive the ARI and dramatically improve reading achievement by our students so they can be successful in all aspects of education?
- Once a student can read well, he/she is much more likely to perform better in other subjects, especially in the critical areas of math, science, and technology. STEM (science, technology, engineering, and mathematics) is critical to Alabama's economic success, and Alabama students must be proficient in STEM-related subjects. As state superintendent of education, what will you do to improve Alabama students' success in STEM-related courses?
- From 2011 to 2015, Alabama's high school graduation rate increased from 72 percent to 89 percent. The Alabama Department of Education released data on the 2015 graduates that revealed only 70 percent of those in the 89 percent graduation rate demonstrated readiness to go to college or were on a pathway toward a career. As state superintendent of education, what will you do to make sure all high school graduates are college- and career-ready?
- Under normal circumstances, educators, parents, and the community usually agree that the better the quality of a school's teaching staff, the better chance each student has to be successful. A way to measure teacher quality is through an annual evaluation. As state superintendent of educa-

tion, what would you do to ensure all Alabama schools are staffed with highly qualified and highly effective teachers and administrators?

- No state in America can experience economic growth without a successful system of public education. Any successful educational system prepares students for success beyond high school, be it a job, continued education, or both. Career and technical education are essential to all students being prepared for life. As state superintendent of education, what would you do to ensure every student is prepared to be a successful graduate, with the requisite skills required to be a strong contributing member of society, and be able to perform successfully in his/her chosen field of work?

Alabama education must improve. As the old saying goes, you're either making progress, stagnant, or losing ground. We join the State Board of Education in wanting public education to make progress. The next generations of Alabama business leaders and employees are being educated now, most of them in public schools.

It is imperative that the candidate who is selected is the very best person to guide and lead our public-school teachers, administrators, and, most importantly, our students to educational success.

William J. Canary is president and CEO of the Business Council of Alabama. Joe Morton PhD is the chairman and president of the Business Education Alliance.

So in the end, the results, no matter what the outcome, should bring a *good tired* and a peace knowing you did the right thing—a basic pillar and principle for leading others.

Yes matters!

Chapter Review Questions

- Do you live by Yoda's philosophy for leading?
- Do you consider yourself to be more of a yes or a no person?
- Why?

- What situation or challenge allowed you to think yes not no?
- Do you worry about making wrong decisions?
- Are you *good tired* in your leadership journey?
- If so, why?
- When were you *bad tired*, what satisfaction did you get from winning?
- What cause were you willing to fight for when you lacked any or little support?
- How does the truth impact the mission?
- Is encouraging dissent a winning strategy?
- What does opinions without facts and facts without opinion mean?

CHAPTER 6

Importance of Failure

Success is
stumbling from
failure to failure
with no loss of
enthusiasm.
Winston Churchill

I've missed more than nine thousand shots in my career. I've lost almost three hundred games. Twenty-six times, I've been trusted to take the game-winning shot and missed. I've failed over and over and over again in my life. And that is why I succeed.

—Michael Jordan

Sir Richard Branson, founder of the Virgin Group, fosters a culture that celebrates and encourages failure. Why? At Virgin, it is a well-held belief that without trying something new and failing, it is nearly impossible to grow and innovate.

> We've never been 100 percent sure that any of the businesses we've started at Virgin were going to be successful. But over forty-five years, we've always stood by our motto: *Screw it, do it.*

Do not be embarrassed by your failures, learn from them, and start again. Making mistakes and experiencing setbacks is part of the DNA of every successful entrepreneur, and I am no exception. (Sir Richard Branson)

Talk about your failures.

Another thing that distinguishes great leaders from average leaders is complete willingness to fail. Risk is a trigger that empowers you to seek excellence. Without a healthy dose of fear and risk you will never achieve excellence.

In the political world, the very best consultants are the ones who remember how they failed and lost, not focusing exclusively on their successes and wins.

So before you celebrate your achievements, acknowledge your failures, which forms another nugget in the leadership toolbox.

In 2017, the United States Chamber of Commerce invited me to participate in a leadership exchange in Israel. I was joined by state and regional chamber executives from all corners of the country.

While in Jerusalem, we had the opportunity to spend time with Saul Singer, one of the authors of *Start-Up Nation: The Story of Israel's Economic Miracle*. *The Atlantic* magazine wrote this about the book, "Dan Senor and Saul Singer have done the impossible. A fascinating and illuminating look at the reasons Israel has become one of the world's prime incubators of technological innovation. An indispensable business book."

How can Israel—with only 7.1 million people, no natural resources, enemies on every border, and in a constant state of war—produce more start-up companies than Japan, India, Korea, Canada, and the United Kingdom? Why does Israel have more companies on the NASDAQ than Japan, Korea, Singapore, India, and all of Europe Combined? The answer is simple.

Singer told us one day in Jerusalem that "there is no suggestion that Israelis are immune from the universally high failure rate of start-ups. But Israeli culture and regulations reflect a unique attitude to failure, one that has managed to repeatedly bring failed entrepreneurs back into the system to constructively use their experience to try again rather than leave permanently stigmatized and marginalized."

He went on to make these points. "It is critical to distinguish between a well-planned experiment and a roulette wheel. In Israel, this distinction is established early in military training. We don't cheerlead you excessively for a good performance, and we don't finish you off permanently for a bad performance."

He noted a 2006 Harvard University study that entrepreneurs who have failed in their previous enterprise have an almost one-in-five chance of success in their next start-up, which is a higher success rate than that for first-time entrepreneurs.

Fascinating how failure is a path to success.

As a leader, I have always done what I believe in, and I have always followed my heart. *Without trial and error and risk-taking, you remain stagnant and predictable, and ultimately, you will become complacent. Risks are about pushing yourself until you are operating outside of your comfort zone.*

Risk-taking is an increasingly critical element of leadership and essential for a leader's effectiveness.

Risk-taking can be defined as "undertaking a task in which there is a lack of certainty or a fear of failure." The problem at the core of risk taking is fear—fear of failure, fear of success, fear of looking like a fool, fear of seeming ignorant, fear of seeming too aggressive.

Taking risks means confronting the fears and challenges and having the courage to move forward. Playing it safe and not taking a risk is probably the most dangerous thing you could do in today's rapidly changing and highly competitive business environment. Reward and profit come in direct proportion to the risk involved. Leaders are ultimately judged on the results that they deliver. Sometimes it can be easy for leaders just to tread water, especially when things seem to be going well. Yet in truth, continued creativity and risk-taking is critical to leadership success.

Leadership success is about finding new or better ways of doing things. Leadership success is about finding different solutions to long-standing problems. Leaders need to be willing to dip their toes into the pool of uncertainty without letting the fear of failure stop them. Leaders who want to achieve success understand that taking risks is an essential part of achieving results. Leaders must discover their "risk tolerance" by stepping out of the comfort zone and engage with these two things in mind:

- Learn from mistakes.
- Recognize that success and failure are connected and are necessary for growth.

Risks are all about encouraging your own development into the best person and professional you can be. If the word *risk* is too strong a word, try instead *thinking ahead of the box.*

So who is Robert Morris, and why is he relevant to this discussion about the importance of failure?

In 1798 at the age of sixty-four, he was sent to debtor's prison for three years. He died in 1806 after being released from prison, living in poverty until the end of his life. So was Robert Morris a failure? Not in the mind of our first president George Washington. Washington believed that as a nation, we could not have waged or, for that matter, won the Revolutionary War without Robert Morris.

So here is the rest of the story. Robert Morris was one of the signers of the Declaration of Independence. He pledged his wealth and life to pursue his dream for a free nation. Robert Morris would be the primary financier of the Revolutionary War.

Results matter!

Most of us don't get it right the second, third, or fourth time either. Winston Churchill said it best, "Success is the ability to go from failure to failure without losing your enthusiasm." Churchill blew one assignment after another until he came up against the big one and saved the world.

There is no such thing as failure. There are only results. (Tony Robbin)

Chapter Review Questions

- Are you managing your failures in an appropriate way?
- How do you balance the ground between being reckless and being proactive after a failure? Is it simply risk versus reward?
- What have you learned from failure in your life?
- Why do some leaders learn from failure and others seem not too?
- Do you believe that if a leader fails, it is because that leader had a failed vison or plan?
- How do you assess the importance of a failure on an organization? What are the metrics?
- Is a lack of fear to fail a good thing?
- When you fail, how do you dust yourself and bounce back with a new strategy?

CHAPTER 7

Thinking Ahead of the Box

My education budget will provide $25 million to expand our nationally recognized First Class Pre-K program. This significant increase will expand the program by 193 classrooms. It will be the largest investment in Alabama First Class Pre-K to date and takes us even closer to providing more of Alabama's youngest learners a strong start.
—Governor Kay Ivey,
State of the State Address, March 5, 2019

Generally, people are afraid to get outside their comfort zone, and the rules that have governed them—growth and creativity—become the victim of this thinking.

Are these just wishful headlines or an example of leadership thinking ahead of the box?

- Investing in early childhood education reaps benefits for a lifetime!
- Alabama business leaders agree that increasing the education investment in our youngest children is and will be a top state priority!
- It is in the best interest of business to invest in quality early education since business is the greatest consumer of our education system!

The key as a leader is to challenge and invite your team to think visually. I adapted a practice that whenever we were confronted with a major challenge, I would open my notebook and, on a blank piece of paper (with a black Sharpie), draw a box or a triangle, outlining a game plan to encourage all views about how a solution could take a new path for this problem. We would make copies of my primitive drawings to use as a platform for our plan of action.

So we did make more progress than anyone ever imagined. We looked at things differently, encouraged nonconformity, challenged the status quo, and asked the question: Why not?

My definition of being *ahead of the box*.

How did we change the world in Alabama for the better?

It all began when I invited former *Miami Herald* publisher David Lawrence Jr., an early childhood education advocate who was instrumental in passing a statewide constitutional amendment to provide prekindergarten for all four-year-olds in Florida, to address the board of directors of the Business Council of Alabama in 2007.

He had an incredible message that said if we invest in education for our children at an early age, not only will they excel but as adults, they also will be more productive citizens. The challenge and mission that David offered us was an incredibly enlightening experience for our board members.

In Alabama, it was like a light switched on. As a business advocacy organization, we knew that the future of economic success and prosperity depended on the education we provide for our children.

But building momentum for early childhood education took leadership, planning, and teamwork on the part of BCA.

In 2009, we hosted a business leadership summit on early childhood investment with Robert Dugger, Sara Watson, Phil Dotts BCA's Volunteer Leader (an early childhood advocate from before day one) and Governor Bob Riley.

Dugger, an investment manager, and Watson were significant players in the Pew Charitable Trusts' Partnership for America's Economic Success.

The summit brought together business, education, and child-education advocates for a full day of planning for action. This collaboration would establish prekindergarten as a fundamental foundation for adequate early childhood development in Alabama.

We knew this effort had to be broader than just the BCA.

After that day, Governor Riley announced his plans to expand voluntary prekindergarten education in Alabama.

Who was Bob Riley?

He was a leader beyond competition and a charismatic personality only akin to Ronald Reagan, in my opinion. Riley served three terms as a member of the United States Congress before becoming Alabama's fifty-second governor, an office he held from 2003 to 2011. As a popular congressman, he made and kept a self-imposed term limit promise, which expired in 2002. He returned to Alabama, ran for and won the governor's seat, and will likely go down in history as the state's most successful chief executive.

Under his watch, Alabama made great gains in what I refer to as the "Three Es"—education, economic development, and ethics.

His courage, understanding, and vision to join with BCA as a champion of both pre-K and early childhood development remains, perhaps, his most lasting and important legacy. I was privileged to share a political foxhole with him on this and other critical policy initiatives during his nearly three thousand days in office.

Riley has been a very special mentor, friend, and blessing in my life. We continue to visit, exchange ideas, and plot to change the world.

My only regret is that we never went to Iowa and entered him in the nation's first primary caucus for president.

The "First Class" statewide rollout started small, but each year, the legislature would add additional funding and more classrooms. And today, it remains rated the best pre-K program in the nation by the National Institute for Early Education Research for its high-quality standards.

As president and CEO of the BCA, I gave more than forty speeches a year throughout Alabama and four or five outside the state. A common theme was always early childhood education, pre-K, and career readiness.

The facts and benefits of early childhood education speak for themselves: Every $1 spent on high-quality pre-K creates $7 to $9 in future savings to the communities and states that invest. Children with quality early learning opportunities are more likely to read at grade level, graduate from high school, earn more money, and contribute more tax dollars.

This is a win-win scenario for everyone.

We simply decided to construct and lead a movement just as builders who work with mortar and stone use pillars to support a structure from the foundation up.

In the end, we simply believed that no person stands taller than when he or she bends over to pick up a child.

Proving the impossible to be possible is the epitome of leadership. To encourage your team to try new things and achieve big goals, you need to take on those seemingly impossible challenges yourself.

Show others how to think *outside the box* and demonstrate to your team that hard work pays off and innovation is valued.

Just draw that box and think *ahead of the box*!

Early Childcare Has $1 billion Economic
Impact and Long-Lasting Business Benefits

Alabama's early childcare and education
might be a $1-billion industry that creates 25,000
jobs; but it has far-reaching effects on business,
families, and society, according to a new study
released Monday (http://www.smartstartalabama.
org/news/?newsID=37&date=12/16/2013).

The study conducted by Auburn University
at Montgomery for the Alabama Partnership for
Children says that early care and education rank
among the top industries in economic impact
and the number of jobs created. The study by
AUM economic professor Keivan Deravi says
the industry has a $1.03-billion state impact and
is responsible for an average 24,717 full-time
equivalent jobs. Perhaps a greater influence is on
society: early education leads to better personal
and financial outcomes throughout a man or
woman's life. Jeremy Arthur, president and CEO
of the Chamber of Commerce Association of
Alabama, spoke at the news conference at AUM.

The CCAA and the Business Council of
Alabama ten years ago formed The Partnership,
a strategic alliance that doubles their individual
influence and works for an educated workforce,
among other goals, he said. "Economic development and education are what the business community focuses on," Arthur said.

He compared the impact of the early childhood education industry and the aerospace
industry that has 36,000 direct jobs and the
state's automotive industry with 34,000 direct
jobs. "It's a significant job creator and is also a
significant workforce," said Arthur.

The BCA, a member of the Alabama School Readiness Alliance (http://alabamaschoolreadiness.org/), is a strong supporter of early childhood education and of expanding Alabama's voluntary prekindergarten program for four-year-olds. BCA president and CEO William J. Canary serves on the ASRA Pre-K Taskforce and advocates investment in a product that will "increase sales, establish a foundation for future growth, and bear dividends for decades."

"Every $1 spent on high-quality pre-K programs creates $7 to $9 in future savings to the communities and states that invest," Canary said earlier this year when the legislature appropriated an additional $9.4 million to expand pre-K to an additional 1,500 children.

The program is administered by certifiably trained staff. Deravi, the study's author, said no other investment will have as much impact in the long run as early childhood education. "It absolutely generates an enormous rate of return," Deravi said.

Calvin Moore Jr., director of childcare services for the Alabama Department of Human Resources, said childcare is a struggle for many families that have to juggle work and children. "No family should have to choose between high-quality care and their right to a wonderful career," he said.

Gail Piggott is executive director of the Alabama Partnership for Children (http://www.smartstartalabama.org/). "There are not many investments that you can make that have a $1-billion impact on our economy and employ 25,000 and allow tens of thousands of parents to go to work," she said.

> *The BCA, Alabama's foremost voice for business, is a nonpartisan, statewide business association representing the interests and concerns of nearly one million working Alabamians through its member companies and its partnership with the Chamber of Commerce Association of Alabama. The BCA is Alabama's exclusive affiliate to the US Chamber of Commerce and the National Association of Manufacturers.* (Dana Beyerle)
>
> Business Council of Alabama

It has been suggested that Albert Einstein may have said, "If at first the idea is not absurd, then there is no hope for it."

Chapter Review Questions

- What does "think ahead of the box" mean to you?
- Can you draw a picture a box or triangle of your challenge and a plan of action to solve it from a blank piece of paper?
- What does "take on the status quo" mean to you?
- How does thinking ahead of the box impact leadership?
- Can you write a paragraph about your experience when you lead ahead of that box?

CHAPTER 8

Navigating a Crisis

*Faith and fear both demand that you believe in
something that you cannot see. You choose.*

—Bob Proctor

The magic in becoming a great leader is to predict the future, not
to reward the past. Every organization faces the problem of how to
identify the people who are most likely to lead through growing com-
plexity, uncertainty, and change. There is a big difference between
managing a crisis and leading during a crisis.

Leading during a crisis implies that you have a destination in
mind and that you will bring the organization to that destination.
Leaders create events that will bring all to that destination in a time
of crisis.

Tools in a crisis:

- Getting all to understand the vision behind a plan
- Ability to execute the plan incorporating the actionable steps to achieve the plan and not becoming distracted
- Communicating that plan in a clear and meaningful way
- Staying on focus

Emotions in the moment of a crisis, such as fear or loyalty, will pull you in a direction; but your job is to remain focused, set objectives that benefit all, and stay the course.

Navigating a Crisis

- ✓ Embrace the trouble.
- ✓ Know where you need to end up.
- ✓ Know the facts and accept them.
- ✓ The truth always comes out.
- ✓ Stay calm.
- ✓ Remember things usually get worse before they get better.
- ✓ You will know when and why to walk away.
- ✓ Trust yourself.

Crises occur irrespective of one's fame, power, or prestige—deal with it. Good stuff, bad stuff. (Judy Smith)

Who is Judy Smith?

I first met Judy Smith when we were both working in the White House under President George H. W. Bush. Judy joined the staff as deputy press secretary in 1992, and I would reconnect with her more than two decades later when she was invited to appear at the Business Council's summer governmental conference and stole the show.

Interestingly, Judy Smith along with my life-long friend Judy Retchin (my next-door neighbor growing up in Babylon, Long Island

N.Y.) were both Assistant U. S. Attorneys who were the prosecutors in the drug trial of D.C. Mayor Marion Barry. In 1992, Judy (Retchin) was appointed to the bench of the Superior Court of the District of Columbia by President George H.W. Bush. Best known in the media as the "Fixer," Judy Smith is a world-renowned crisis management expert who serves as founder and CEO of Smith & Company, a strategic advisory firm considered to be one of the top crisis firms in the world.

For more than twenty-five years, she has served as an adviser for a host of corporate, celebrity, nonprofit, and government clients, providing strategic counsel to help individuals and organizations navigate challenging issues.

Her groundbreaking work inspired the hit TV show *Scandal*; and her book, *Good Self, Bad Self: How to Bounce Back from a Personal Crisis*, incorporated years of experience to help readers develop the tools to face a crisis and navigate through it.

Little did I know how much I would rely upon her counsel in 2018 when reality forced me to confront my own significant crisis.

Case Study

In this case study we will examine *me*. This is my personal journey in navigating a crisis.

The overriding question for me was, "Does adversity build character?"

Trust me. It does.

Most leaders must, at some point, stand up to adversity. Great leaders have a direct relationship with character, and that is why character has always been the foundation for leadership.

Little did I know how much adversity I was about to be confronted with and the impact it would have upon so many people.

Jo Bonner was the US representative for Alabama's first congressional district from 2001 to 2013. He resigned from Congress to accept a position with the University of Alabama, served as Chief of Staff to Alabama governor Kay Ivey before becoming the president of the University of South Alabama. I am blessed to call him my friend.

Jo wrote these words to me in 2017: "BCA is now doing things and providing leadership that only a few short years ago we didn't do. We'll never win every race but will surely lose if we sit idly on the sidelines and don't challenge the status quo!"

Those words helped me to better understand the crisis that was about to overwhelm me and place me somewhere between a bullet and a target.

I was committed, along with my organization, to change the political world in Alabama, which made many powerful institutions, many powerful individuals, and an existing institutional political machine very unhappy.

So what happened?

As a direct result of the efforts that BCA spearheaded in 2010, the Alabama of 2018 had the most pro-business legislature in its history, and our group was enjoying more influence than at any other time since its founding in 1985. We had recruited, funded, and elected slates of legislative candidates who themselves were small business owners and had the experience of signing the front of a paycheck so others could sign the back. Legislative committees that once passed anti-business bills with conveyor-belt efficiency in earlier days were now approving BCA's pro-business measures with similar regularity.

BCA, for example, had drafted and passed a constitutional amendment declaring Alabama a right-to-work state, which essentially removed the threat of widespread unionization within our borders, and we successfully amended legislation that would have allowed employees the unfettered right to carry firearms in the workplace.

In such a pro-business environment of our own creation, it was surprising to hear distance drumbeats of discontent from the upper floors of a number of corporate buildings.

Little did I know that our great and celebrated success in overturning the political applecart in Alabama would lead to an accelerated exit from BCA in 2018.

PART 1
Background

Here is the story, the background, and the plan to initially navigate this crisis.

On May 21, 2018, the executive committee of the BCA met to create a plan of action for its future governance and transition. BCA never had a "succession plan" to replace its president and CEO, and frankly, it had not made transitions work well throughout its more than thirty years of existence.

My goal was to change that history and fulfill the terms of my contract, a contract that would be in force until December 31, 2019.

This plan would include establishing strategic goals that would ensure unity for the business community as it needed to participate in both the 2018 and 2020 election cycles and the 2019 legislative session.

Over the years, the BCA has not been immune from attacks. In a 2004 missive, former Alabama Education Association executive secretary Paul Hubbert posed the question, "Does BCA speak for business anymore?" AEA was then a powerful union representing tens of thousands of education workers in Alabama.

This line of attack was a result of the BCA standing up to the status quo's political establishment that had been entrenched for decades. Many opposing entities understood that BCA would not relent, and they continued to resort to extreme lengths to undermine the organization and its leadership.

This manifested itself in many different forms over the years, ranging from threats of economic sanctions to the threat of an active takeover in both 2017 and 2018.

False information was disseminated by political bloggers making several erroneous claims. Paid bloggers targeted personal attacks on our leadership and me. We made it clear that we would not be intimidated into bad decision-making. I was often reminded that when you are relevant, you put yourself in the crosshairs.

I never thought that my leadership style and personality would need to be defended. But it did. BCA chairman Perry Hand put out this statement in an attempt to deflect the falsehoods and the attacks:

> Billy Canary's tenure as president and CEO of the BCA is unparalleled in both his ability to take the BCA to the next level, as well as his ability to coalesce the business community, build unique partnerships in the business community, and build one of the largest political war chests in the state. Along the way, he has put together a great staff that has proven themselves over and over. The executive committee is extremely pleased with Billy Canary's accomplishments for BCA over these past fifteen years. Billy and we are committed to a "succession plan" that will provide for an orderly transition of leadership.
>
> That's what good CEOs do. Only the unthoughtful and the uninitiated would recommend the removal of a very successful leader without the proper planning in place to provide for the transition of leadership. BCA will not risk all we've accomplished to secure relief from bloggers and political pundits.

One principle remained constant during this crisis—the BCA's guiding force was just as important in 2018 as when it was first created in 1985. Its mission was then, and remains today, to create a vibrant economic climate, an educated workforce, to lead with bold ideas, take on the big fights, and win the future for the business community.

We used our seat at the policy, regulatory, and legislative tables to lead on those matters that were important to our members.

Fresh ideas drove productive and realistic solutions to achieve concrete results on our pro-growth agenda.

Innovative new ideas were put forth through the strength of our partnership with the chambers of commerce, our coalitions, and subject matter experts.

BCA did not shrink from challenges, but rather, we confronted them and overcame them. In Alabama, we were the largest advocacy business organization representing small, large, and emerging businesses.

BCA consistently fought against unions, numerous anti-business elected officials, the trial bar, and special interest groups that attempted to threaten job creation or job growth.

What Winston Churchill once said best encapsulated the integrity of the BCA throughout its thirty-three-year history: "You have enemies? Good. That means you've stood up for something sometime in your life."

And did I have enemies.

Now I found myself along with our volunteer leadership in the midst of a full-blown crisis. Riding it out was not an option.

One upside of a crisis is to use the moment to examine yourself and your willingness to put into practice all that you often preached about fighting for what was right no matter the cost.

I tried to confront the challenges and challengers. It was my instinct and my passion. However, the end result should be a willingness to change direction, if necessary, and take responsibility for your own actions. Be willing to admit your failings and be honest about them.

So I addressed the BCA's executive committee in April 2018 with the intent of bringing the crisis to an end and resolving the issues at its root.

At least I thought I could.

PART 2

The Crisis in Real Time

My Statement to the Executive Committee of the BCA—Dealing with the Crisis in Real-Time (April 2018)

I thank both the officers and the members of this executive committee for allowing me this opportunity to address you this morning. I want to thank our chairman, Perry Hand, for his incredible leadership during this period in BCA's thirty-three-year history.

Today you will collectively conduct an open dialogue about your views and vision for BCA today and in the future.

I know that you share a mutual agenda to bring success, integrity, and openness to solve problems while moving Alabama forward.

As a business advocacy organization, we continue to look to the future to create a climate in Alabama for new and existing businesses to locate or expand.

Past success is no guarantee, but it does demonstrate how a *united* business community can accomplish worthwhile and satisfactory goals. By coming together today, your mission is to simply discuss how we can make this organization better, stronger, and most effective for *all* our members and the near one million Alabamians employed by those member companies.

My tenure began at BCA with a simple question: "How will *you* bring BCA to the next level, as well as create a plan of action to coalesce the business community, build unique partnerships in the business community, balance the BCA budget, eradicate the debt [millions of dollars in 2003], build one of the largest political war chests in the state, and finally, how will you assemble and create a staff that is second to none?"

The challenge then is different from today.

Then, we fought for relevancy. This shifted to *first* to *effective* to *success*, and now we are *significant*.

I have love for two families in my life: the Canary family and this BCA family. Both are my passion, and I have a committed desire to protect them with my life!

I want both of those families to enjoy success, respect, and financial security while commencing into a wonderful new future. Both deserve nothing less.

When I contemplated the political landscape around BCA's role in one of my very first interviews, I likened the political process in 2003 to a *cold war*. The superpowers were AEA, gaming interests, and trial lawyers.

It turned into a contest primarily between BCA, Paul, Milton, and Jerry for the political and economic domination of Alabama.

It was a massive contest between political and economic ideologies, and it was "fought" by propaganda in the press and with dollars to control our government and our courts. And in my not-so-humble opinion, I was the right person to take on that battle.

But fifteen years later, the Iron Curtain has lifted, and that cold war has come to an end. So today we have an opportunity for restructuring.

In BCA's thirty-three-year history, we have *never* enjoyed an orderly transition, including a time certain for that transition.

I have been given the privilege to serve fifteen-plus years at the helm, becoming the longest serving president and CEO in BCA's thirty-three-year history. I have a desire to be the first to leave on favorable terms.

Life is about seasons. My contract says that season ends on December 31, 2020.

I have learned it is always best to leave when many want you to stay. That was the case for me upon three major departures in my life: elected office in New York, the White House, and the American Trucking Associations.

When I left the American Trucking Associations as its president and CEO on my journey to BCA, a national transportation trade magazine wrote this about me:

> Canary's tenure will surely be best remembered for his building of bridges between the national organization and its state affiliates and councils. It was his top priority.
>
> During his tenure, he helped restore a full measure of trust, which had frayed under the pressures of ATA's restructuring, between the national federation, its councils and state trucking associations. He put it all back together the direct opposite of the Humpty Dumpty rhyme.
>
> Despite economic hard times and the events of 9/11, ATA has grown in strength and influence. It is one of the measurable outcomes of Canary's stewardship. As a result, Governor Graves will inherit a stronger more powerful ATA.

This was written in part from an editorial entitled, *Passing the Baton.*

That is the way one wants to leave and the proper way to create an orderly transition if you truly love an organization. I loved ATA, and I love BCA.

BCA's guiding force is as important today as when first envisioned in 1985 when the BCA was created.

As the most relevant and effective business advocacy association in Alabama, during my tenure, we have worked every day to create a vibrant economic climate, financial stability, coalitions, partnerships, and the strength to *always* punch back with honesty and integrity.

These are the keys to creating and sustaining a legacy for BCA's future. This morning, you meet not to litigate the past but to embrace the promise of its future.

I love BCA. And I want those assembled here—our governing structure, BCA's executive committee—to finish today's discussion and formally resolve to make BCA stronger, financially secure, and stand *united* as Alabama's business community!

For me, I am reminded of those powerful words spoken by Lou Gehrig's in Yankee Stadium on July 4: "Yet today I consider myself the luckiest man on the face of this earth."

I feel the same.

One of the other significant achievements for BCA over the years has been an ability to identify women and men from all segments of Alabama's economy to lead this organization to invest hundreds and hundreds of hours of service to BCA—women and men willing to put individual interests aside for what is in the collective best interest of Alabama's business community and BCA. The epitome of true leadership.

And future evidence of our significance, we do have a staff second to none—*always making the impossible seem easy.*

I am blessed to have the love of my family and the friendship of so many. Thank you for the privilege to serve 5,517 days as BCA's president and CEO. It remains far from over. But let us put forth a plan for BCA's future, today and now. I am reminded of the words of Theodore Roosevelt in reflecting upon those 5,517 days: "Far and away the best prize that life offers are the chance to work hard at work worth doing."

Thank you.

PART 3

The Plan-Transition and Succession

Business Council of Alabama
(BCA)
Transition and Succession
By
William Canary

2018–2020
Succession/Transition and Unity Planning
Business Council of Alabama (BCA)

✓ BCA's orderly transition, including a time certain for the announcement and a celebration of fifteen-plus years at the helm (becoming the longest-serving president and CEO in BCA's thirty-three-year history and the first to leave on "successful" terms)

✓ BCA chairman, officers, and executive committee to encourage, enlighten, and provide counsel on *transition unity* and *succession* to the entire BCA leadership (board of directors, staff and membership) securing an understanding for the benefit of all parties (BCA and entire business community) for an orderly and planned succession and transition

Action Items

- The release and announcement of a succession and transition plan
- Appointment by the chairman forming a BCA Presidential and CEO Transition and Selection Committee 2018–2020
- All to be approved, adopted, and voted upon the executive committee prior to August 11
- Date certain for the announcement and selection of the (future) BCA president and CEO

Business Council of Alabama
President and CEO
Specific Duties and Responsibilities

The president and CEO will be responsible for specific results and will

- Manage/motivate/direct the association staff; provide leadership for the staff in the planning and execution of BCA's policies and programs.
- Lead BCA's political/advocacy agenda.
- Enhance the council's value to its members (ROI).
- Lead a strategic planning process that positions BCA to effectively deal with emerging and changing trends and needs of the Alabama business community.
- Create an agenda that attracts and sustains strategic CEO membership involvement.
- Strive to achieve unity, where possible, within the membership on key issues affecting the business community.
- Build and direct results-oriented teams that deliver specific results in the legislative, regulatory, and technical education arenas.
- Execute the policies established by the board to advance the interests of the council.
- Anticipate the political, social, and economic issues that will affect the BCA and recommend appropriate action and/or response as may be necessary to government agencies, the membership, and the public.
- Work with the chief executive officers, corporate staffs, office heads, and all leaders of the member companies to advance their goals and agenda.
- Serve as the business community's key spokesperson before all appropriate venues and audiences.
- Work with the appropriate association heads and Alabama "thought leaders" to build coalitions on key issues.

PART 4

Leadership's Response to the Challengers

As you know, we have worked diligently to address the concerns and issues you have raised; however, we have not, in good conscience, been able to adhere to the deadline dates you have prescribed to our executive committee.

I invited you to address our executive committee on April 10 where you voiced several concerns related to the BCA leadership. You asked that the committee remove our president and CEO by May 1 or June 1. The committee did not concur but did instruct the chairman to create a transition and succession plan. Over the next month, that work ensued; and the transition and succession plan was adopted on May 21, 2018, at a meeting of the executive committee.

On June 4, 2018, I, along with BCA's first vice chairman and second vice chairman, met with you and a small group of business leaders that you assembled, and we presented this plan to you.

Following that meeting, I was sent your list of demands. I have worked to find areas of compromise, but you have made it clear that compromising is not an option.

The BCA executive committee will be meeting on June 21, 2018, to approve details of the transition plan adopted on May 21 with the goal of having a new CEO installed no later than January 1, 2019. We will be appointing members of the selection committee, and their work is to commence immediately.

Our goal of conducting an orderly and thoughtful transition in executive leadership, which has never been achieved in the history of BCA, remains. The full BCA board of directors will be apprised of this work at a meeting on June 25, 2018.

Throughout this time period, this internal debate has played out in public with paid political bloggers launching false statements and defamatory rhetoric, hoping to interfere with these orderly discussions.

Our organization will not allow these personal attacks to alter our course for an orderly transition of executive leadership at BCA. We will continue our work with respect and thoughtful diligence.

As you know, BCA's membership is broad and diverse, representing the interests and concerns of nearly one million working Alabamians through its member companies that include businesses of all sizes and virtually every segment of Alabama's business community—from manufacturing to retail, agriculture to financial services, and many, many more.

The BCA is also Alabama's exclusive representative to the National Association of Manufacturers and the US Chamber of Commerce. Given this broad and diverse constituency, it is even more important that an orderly transition of leadership be conducted. We have worked diligently to try and address each and every concern you have presented.

As a business advocacy organization, we continue to look to the future to create a climate in Alabama for new and existing businesses to locate or expand.

Past success is no guarantee, but it does demonstrate how a united business community can accomplish worthwhile and satisfactory goals. Our door remains open to you and all Alabama businesses that wish to move our state forward.

Thank you for the support given to the BCA in the past, and I truly hope that our actions in the coming weeks will justify your support once again.

Generally, the education you have received should have given you one gift in particular—the ability for critical thought.

Do not ignore the common things, the day-to-day activities upon which we build our lives.

It is these small changes, these little differences, that add up to make the changes that reorder society and create new orders.

And never believe that doing everyday tasks properly doesn't matter. George Washington Carver summed it up best when he said. "When you can do the common things of life in an uncommon way, you will command the attention of the world."

In your leadership journey, you have had faith to surround yourself with others who have shared your convictions, beliefs, work ethic, and all the other tenets that are the outward manifestation of faith.

The education and lessons learned in your role as a leader in your journey will serve you for a lifetime.

PART 5
Falling Forward

As my friend, Judy Smith, once told me, "And to all the people who have made mistakes, screwed up, or found themselves in a situation they didn't create, and for those who face a crisis or find themselves in a situation they never anticipated, may you know that there is a way through it and a second act waiting on the other side."

BCA's Canary Announces Departure,
Accepts Position at US Chamber
For immediate release: July 6, 2018

MONTGOMERY, Alabama—Business Council of Alabama President and CEO William J. Canary announced today that he is leaving the BCA and has accepted a position as senior fellow at the US Chamber of Commerce.

"I am announcing today that I am retiring from my position as president and CEO of the Business Council of Alabama to pursue an opportunity as senior fellow at the US Chamber of Commerce," said Canary. "It has been my great privilege to lead the BCA these past fifteen years. During my tenure, we have worked every day to make the BCA the most relevant and effective business advocacy association in Alabama. It has been an honor to work alongside men and women from all segments of Alabama's economy, who invest hundreds and hundreds of hours of volunteer service to the BCA, for what is in the collective best interest of Alabama's business community."

"Billy Canary is the longest serving president and CEO in BCA's thirty-three-year history, and I commend him for his exceptional service to the Business Council of Alabama over these last fifteen years," said BCA chairman Perry Hand. "From day 1, Billy has worked to create partnerships, both statewide and nationally, that have served our organization and Alabama's business community well. Billy has an incredible background having worked at the White House, the Republican National Committee, and the American Trucking Associations, to name a few, and he will be difficult to replace. We at the BCA remain committed to coalescing the Alabama business community for the betterment of our state and our state's economy."

"The BCA has achieved major successes through the years under the leadership of Billy Canary and the entire team at the BCA," said 2017 BCA chairman Jeff Coleman.

"There is definitely more work to do, which is why the BCA is focused on being a catalyst to bring growth and prosperity to our great state. We are currently in the middle of an election year that will see a new legislature elected a legislature that will have to develop effective solutions for infrastructure, education, and health care, to name a few.

"As an organization that respectfully represents over one million working Alabamians, we are strongly committed to the work ahead of us to move Alabama forward." During the interim, BCA chief of staff and senior vice president for governmental affairs Mark Colson have been assigned the day-to-day duties of president."

The Business Council of Alabama is Alabama's foremost voice for business. The BCA is a nonpartisan statewide business association representing the interests and concerns of nearly one million working Alabamians through its member companies and its partnership with the Chamber of Commerce Association of Alabama. The BCA is Alabama's exclusive affiliate to the US Chamber of Commerce and the National Association of Manufacturers.

I had a choice to make and I choose wisely.

I placed my family, the BCA volunteer leadership, and BCA organization first. It would prove to be the right decision and a way to end the crisis.

In the end, it is all about the process. It is all about giving it your best shot every day. Falling forward means not dwelling on the negative. Step out and speak positive. You may not even believe them right now, but that doesn't matter. Your positive words are changing things for the better.

> Perpetual optimism is a force multiplier. The ripple effect of a leader's enthusiasm and optimism is awesome. (Colin Powell)

Chapter Review—Navigating a Crisis

- ✓ Embrace the trouble.
- ✓ Know where you need to end up.
- ✓ Know the facts and accept them.
- ✓ The truth always comes out. Stay calm.
- ✓ Remember things usually get worse before they get better.
- ✓ You will know when and why to walk away.
- ✓ Trust yourself.

Chapter Questions

- When you find yourself in the "eye of a crisis," how does this list help you prepare for the best in the midst of the worst?
- Is there anything you would add or delete from this list?

- What crisis has most challenged your leadership or leadership opportunities?
- How would you create your plan if faced with crisis?
- Do you have a Judy Smith in your life?
- If not, why not?
- What would falling forward look like to you?
- If you had to reorder this list, how would you do so?

CHAPTER 9

Ringing the Bell

To be a realist you must believe in miracles.
—David Ben Gurion

Leadership is influence.

No matter what the circumstances are that lie before you, embrace the journey you are on, even if it might not be the plan. Many times, your influence is a direct result of your attitude; and finding courage, even when fear might dominate the moment, can greatly influence others who are watching.

A key to leadership in adversity is believing that you can have a positive impact in the immediate world you are living in at the moment. This is what you have been called to do and what you have trained yourself to do all of your life. In the end, you don't need to be a president, CEO, or CFO of an organization to be called to influence those in your life.

Seize the moment, bury fear, and lead by example.

On August 5, 2019, I was having a great day—at least until 11:15 a.m. when my world came to a screeching halt. I went in for my annual physical exam and was both surprised and shocked when I was told with near certainty that I had prostate cancer. Both a blood test and digital exam established significant red flags, according to my physician. When I left my internist's office in a bit of a mental fog, I simply sat in my car and prayed. I prayed for strength. I prayed for my family. I spoke these words from Exodus 14:14: "The Lord will fight for you; you need only to be calm," and prayed, "Lord, please include my healing in your will."

As it neared noon, I drove home.

On my return home, I found my daughter, Margaret, and wife, Leura, having lunch. Margaret was about to begin her senior year at the University of St. Andrews in Scotland and was finishing her summer internship with a local law firm. I asked Leura if I could talk to her for a moment.

We retreated to another room where I told her the results of my physical. Leura, who is ever an optimist, said that until I had a biopsy, it was still a "maybe," but if my physician proved correct, she would travel on the journey with me every step of the way.

On October 3, I discovered that God had a new plan for me. *I had cancer.*

Leura and I immediately called our children. Margaret had, by that time, returned to Scotland for her final year of studies; and our son, Will—a graduate from Sewanee, The University of the South— was living in Birmingham and employed as a financial analyst with a commercial real estate firm.

My message to them was simple—"I love you, and together we will kick ass!"

One of my very best friends and someone I love like a brother is Charles Nailen. We first met in 2003, when he served on the search committee that selected me to serve as president and CEO of the Business Council of Alabama.

A very successful businessman, CPA, and devoted family man, the title of which he is most proud is being "right with God." Charles is a cancer survivor whose prostate cancer was first discovered in 2003, when he was fifty-three.

Statistically, less than 2 percent of those diagnosed with prostate cancer are under the age of fifty-five. So one week after my annual physical and collective "red flags" and before my biopsy, he wrote a five-page letter of inspiration, along with recommending twelve books on the subjects of prostate cancer, faith, and hope to me.

Charles wrote, in part,

> Billy, my cancer was a life-changing positive experience. And I know it will be for you too. It helped me refocus on the things that are really important in life.
> I like the motto adopted by Lance Armstrong shortly after his cancer diagnosis—now there are no more bad days, just *good* days and *great* days. With that mindset, you really try to make every day count.

And he would go on to write,

> You remember that story that's been around a long time about one set of footprints in the sand? It is so true. That happened to me. And you'll find it happening to you. There will be one set of footprints a lot during the next few months. Billy, as I told you before, it's all about *mindset*. Keep a positive attitude in the midst of all this. It will be good for you, and it will be good for those that love you.

Wow! Now you know why I love him.

On October 9, I began treatment. I placed my faith in the hands of God and with my world-class medical team at UAB. I was at peace and was able to focus on my treatment while never looking back.

I was blessed to be able to get the very best medical care at UAB Medicine, which is one of the top academic medical centers in the nation and a recognized leader in quality patient care, research, and training.

My doctor at UAB was John Fiveash, a nationally known specialist who is the leader in his field in treating the specific type of prostate cancer I had. His research interests include clinical trials of novel therapeutics in combination with radiation therapy particularly in the treatment of brain and prostate tumors. As the residency director, he has established online educational opportunities for residents and students to better enable more efficient learning in radiation and oncology. He attended and graduated from Medical College of Georgia, having more than twenty-eight years of diverse experience, especially in radiation oncology. He serves as a professor at the Radiation and Oncology School of Medicine at UAB and senior vice chair for academic programs along with the outstanding educator, endowed chair Robert Y. Kim.

This is the guy you want, and I was blessed to have him!

Dr. Fiveash outlined the three approaches for my cancer treatment. First, beginning on that day, androgen deprivation therapy (ADT for two years), hormones, and Lupron. Second, radiation would begin on January 21, 2020, and conclude after twenty-eight treatments on February 27. Third, six cycles of chemotherapy (Taxotere) with three weeks between each infusion—and all of this in the face of the coronavirus pandemic that was disrupting the globe.

I placed my faith in the hands of God and with my world-class medical team at UAB. I was at peace and was able to focus on my treatment while never looking back.

The chemo road I traveled at times felt like I was run over by a truck.

Lack of energy after an infusion, fatigue, nausea, vomiting, and water retention were commonplace, and by my third infusion, all my hair was gone. By September 16, I had retained more than fifty pounds of water weight through acute edema; but with the help of my internist, Dr. Rakel Patel, I lost fifty-four pounds by November.

Ringing the Bell

After you complete your final radiation and chemo treatment, you are invited to *ring the bell*. It is thought that the tradition began in Texas at the world-famous MD Anderson Cancer Clinic in 1996.

As the story goes, a rear admiral in the US Navy, Irve Le Moyne, was undergoing radiation therapy for head and neck cancer.

He told his doctor that he planned to follow a navy tradition of ringing a bell to signify *when the job was done.* He brought a brass bell to his last treatment, rang it several times, and left it as a donation. It was mounted on a wall plaque in the main building's Radiation Treatment Center with the inscription

> Ringing out
> Ring this bell
> Three times well
> Its toll to clearly say
> My treatment's done
> This course is run
> And I am on my way!
> (Irve Le Moyne)

While I waited to be called back for one of my twenty-eight radiation treatments, which I would commonly call being *zapped*, I would sometimes hear the sound of other patients ringing the bell. It always lifted my spirits. Halfway through my radiation treatments, a young eleven-year-old girl by the name of Ava had a turn to ring the bell, which touched me to my core.

I met Ava and her mother, Amber, during the early stages of my radiation treatments and enjoyed our visits preparing to be *zapped.* Ava was my hero.

She displayed courage, demonstrated her faith in real time, inspired me, and always had enough humor to make life manageable. She taught me that attitude is truly the key to life.

I learned she loved horses just like my daughter. Margaret, a member of the St. Andrews University (UK) polo club, had left behind a wool cap with the university logo on it, so I asked her if I could give it to Ava as a gift from one horse lover to another (Margaret is simply amazing. Fearless caring, loving, smart, adventurous and loyal with an extra dosage of integrity. She loves life, lives life and as I tell her, she will ALWAYS be my baby).

Margaret said, "Absolutely, but only if you send me a picture."

February, even in Alabama, can be cold, and the loss of one's hair makes it even colder. So covering your head with "something" was mandatory. Leura wrapped the wool cap with the perfection that she can bring to all things wonderful, and I made the presentation. Ava was thrilled and loved this gift from Margaret.

One night, her mother sent me a text that Ava would be at Children's Hospital of Alabama for yet another chemo infusion, and she asked if I could visit her after my radiation treatment if physically able.

I did not need to be asked twice.

When I visited, I brought Ava her favorite beverage, an eight-pack of Dr. Pepper. Mr. Chemo decided to challenge her in all ways possible, but he would learn he picked the wrong person. Ava's mother and aunt were with her, and I sat in a chair next to her bed rail and quietly prayed, "Lord, we hold up Ava to you. We don't understand the *why* of this, but someday we will. I know that you love Ava. My prayer is that through all the pain that she and her mother now feel that you provide the warmth of your love and your loving arms around them.

"I pray that you will continue to give this sweet child of yours the courage to face whatever the day throws at her. Thank you for letting me be present in the lives of this family, seeking your healing hand. And it's in your name I pray. *Amen!*"

When I finished praying, her hand appeared from the bed covers, and I held it until she withdrew her hold on me.

I was touched by an angel. That was the moment where I began to understand why I was on this journey.

Ringing the bell after completing twenty-eight radiation treatments and six cycles of chemotherapy was a huge accomplishment for me. Fighting with Mr. Chemo through nausea, exhaustion, edema, water retention, fear, and nerve damage earned me the right of passage to ring the bell.

I felt relief that this day had finally arrived and signaled that the grind of radiation and chemotherapy was over and that I was still standing, albeit barely.

94

So on February 27, I celebrated that I made it through radiation and was joined by my son Will—a caring, kind, thoughtful, loving young man. Will, who works and lives in Birmingham, provided his guest room to me for those twenty-eight radiation treatments.

He showed up for the bell ringing with a four-pack of champagne splits and a glass to offer a toast to all who joined me on this journey toward healing.

That day we also had some eight nurses, technicians, and a very helpful individual, Walter, who ensured I was well-situated with a parking place upon arrival for all my treatments. It was a special moment to have my son with me to celebrate—what a blessing.

But ringing the bell does not always mark the end of your cancer treatment. In my case, the radiation treatments I received for prostate cancer had very few side effects, but the chemotherapy that followed turned out to be rougher. And the ceremony this time around took on a different meaning.

Fatigued and exhausted, feet and hands swollen and numb from water retention, I kept it low-key for the second ringing of the bell, without champagne this time and me barely standing, not able to walk twenty feet while taking a moment to catch my breath.

But still, it was a celebration.

I was celebrating my staying power and ability to get there—the hardest thing I had ever done. But I was mostly just relieved to be done with it and happy to be going home. I drew strength from a personal sense of accomplishment from ringing the bell a second time.

To my oncologist, Dr. Mollie Deshazo, a young gifted, talented, dedicated physician who tells it to you straight and remains deeply committed to her patients' success, failure is not an option. Dr Deshazo is a hero. Giving of herself tirelessly 7/24/365 appreciating the illness by understanding and caring for the whole person. As was the case with Dr. Fiveash, Dr. Deshazo was the physician person you wanted!

This is what she wrote in my medical record on the portal after my first infusion:

> He decided to pursue aggressive therapy. We discussed all the data and the other data that is conflicting on his treatment. He nevertheless wanted to proceed with chemo and voiced an understanding. I advised the patient of the toxicity, including risk of fever, infection, nausea, vomiting, rash, electrolyte abnormalities, allergic infusion reaction, *and complications that could lead to death.* The patient is aware and desired to proceed. His first cycle was complicated by neutropenic fever [which required a seven-hour stay in the emergency room at the height of the COVID-19 pandemic at that time because of a critically low white blood count]. Now receiving Neulasta [white blood count booster] with treatments.

Got to love her for telling you the truth—an absolute blessing!

Because of a very weakened immune system, I sheltered in place at home after each infusion in order to protect myself against the coronavirus.

The pandemic forced upon all of us a new norm of washing hands to the birthday song, social distancing, sheltering in place, wearing masks, and frequent praying. Face-to-face meetings have been replaced by lots of telephoning, emailing, Zoom, and texting! We have learned that our world can change dramatically at any minute.

On November 3, 2020, I received the results of my CT scan. The words I was praying for were pronounced by my oncologist: "Clean and clear."

This journey began thirteen months earlier with a prayer and a verse, Exodus 14:4. I was not alone on this journey. I had legions of friends travel with me, along with world-class medical team, my wife, and my children.

To tell the truth, I am a better person because of cancer.

I took my own advice about leadership: fall forward! And I now learned the true meaning of these words in real time:

No reserves. No retreats. No regrets.

On Mother's Day, after my first chemo infusion and visit to the ER, I sat down and wrote my wife this letter. She deserved to know how much I appreciated her support, love, and friendship as she joined me as my copilot on the journey.

Sunday
May 10, 2020

Dear Leura,

Happy Mother's Day to the world's greatest mother and know you are loved by so, so many. Will and Margaret are truly blessed to be able to call you Mom. You have given them unconditional love and your absolute support no matter the challenge or the opportunity. They are fortunate to have you in their lives and in their DNA. They love you with all their hearts and soul.

Over the past nine months, I know I have asked for so much from you—including an intense pressure to provide for me, counsel me, advocate for me, research everything for me, being there to hold my hand and tell me it will all be alright while never missing a critical appointment or meeting with our medical team.

I want to apologize for all the times my illness made life difficult for you. I'm sorry for all of those times when my concerns scared the sh——out of me and I needed you to be my rock. You were always there for me to provide absolute support love and the ability to tell me it will all be fine. It also has taken me a while to realize this experience might be just as hard for you (or harder) as it is for me.

Because of you, I feel improvements in my body during many days, and I always feel hope. You also see the person you love fighting to be healed and wanting to enjoy life to be with his family for many years to come. *Devoted* is the word that comes to mind when I think of you. It seems like a small word when I think about how much you have done for me. I know you would do anything for me, and you have done everything in your power to help me. I want to thank you for each and every single thing you have done for me, but the list would be too long. I want to thank you for each and every sacrifice you have made for me. You have given to me so selflessly, regardless of what I've been able to give in return. You deserve much more from me. You want things to be easier for me, and I want things to be easier for you. I want you to be happy.

At the same time, I am immensely grateful because I know I would never be able take care of myself as well as you take care of me. I hope you know how amazing you are. It's not easy being married to me; but you have handled it with grace, integrity, and strength.

Anyone else might have walked away, but you're still here for me 24/7/365. I have struggled during this challenge, and I will continue to fight hard. But you are the real hero in this situation. You are behind the scenes working and giving, and that's what has allowed me to fight. There is no one else I could have traveled this journey with, and I wouldn't be here without you. You've taught me what it is to love. You've taught me how to be selfless. You never allowed me to think about giving up. I am healthier because of you. I am stronger because of you. I have hope because of you. I feel loved because of you. I feel closer to God because of you.

I am made whole because of you!

I love you.

Lessons Learned

- People don't care how much you know until they know how much you care.
- In your life journey, you don't need a rearview mirror, just a windshield in the vehicle you choose.
- You can't move people to action unless you first move them with emotion. The heart comes before the head. Kindness is not to be confused with weakness. The past can't be changed.
- Everyone's journey is so very different.

Remember the old adage that happiness is a journey, not a destination.

And *"to be a realist you must believe in* miracles" (David Ben Gurion).

Chapter Review Question

- Write a paragraph describing your miracle?
- And describe how it changed you as a person?
- How did that experience allow you to relate and appreciate others in your life?
- What were the leadership lessons that resulted in this experience?

EPILOGUE: OWN IT

There is no more powerful leadership tool
than your own personal example.
—John Wooden

A Boy with a Dream... "Taking pride in who you are!"

Growing up on Long Island, New York I lived in a wonderfully diverse, multigenerational home that was filled with a potpourri of people who helped shape my life. My immigrant Ukrainian grandparents had a great role in this, as did my other grandmother, my mother and siblings helping to unleash so many things in my life as a young person. In many ways my Ukrainian grandparents were teachers. They taught me that no dream is too big. Never be afraid to stand your ground if you are right. Stay honest and humble. Hard work is a critical skill to succeed and help those who need a hand up.

Lessons that I still carry to this day in both my heart and head. I have had the opportunity to return to the Ukraine numerous times they escaped under Soviet control in search of freedom and the American dream. Given my own personal story, I know that my grandparents drastically underestimated the impact they had on me and the person I became. They nurtured the leader within me helped to unleash it and taught me the value of courage, compassion/love, motivation, and an ability to keep an open mind. A cornucopia of gifts all ground in an understanding of both tradition and kindness.

My father worked in New York City and made the daily trek of commuting more than one hundred miles on the Long Island Railroad, so the time I had with him was most precious. I remember one of those great occasions when he decided I needed some words of wisdom.

I was not sure how to take what he told me. My father said, "Son, four things you need to do in your in life. Marry somebody smarter than you. Always buy quality neckties. Consume all the education you can, and *own it!*"

They didn't sink in at first; but as I have grown older, and hopefully wiser, they have taken root, albeit in a slightly different form. Let me share with you what these maxims have meant to me.

I think he knew that I would have to find somebody smarter than me to survive, but that was not what he meant.

I believe he meant that each of us should surround ourselves with people who constantly stretch our minds and cause us to think critically about the world around us. Offering solutions for the issues we face.

My wife Leura has taught me the importance of having a supporting cast in your life—friends, acquaintances, and contacts—that can help you find the answers for questions through either their input or by forcing you to look deep inside yourself.

> "Close friends are truly life's treasures. Sometimes they know us better than we know ourselves. With gentle honesty, they are there to guide and support us, to share our laughter and our tears. Their presence reminds us that we are never really alone." (Vincent van Gogh)

Quality neckties remind me that some things in our lives should be an outward indication of who we are inward. It's not so much a statement of material consumption, but it's hard to look at a suit or a shirt and know the quality. A tie however, is immediately recognizable. It tells the world that you pay attention to the issues over which you have control, and it reminds you that in the business world especially that your first impression on others is crucial in their perception of you.

My father knew that education is the great advantage in life. Those who have made the sacrifice and dedicated the hours to study that could have been given to play come to know that work is sometimes a reward in itself.

I have seen the value of higher education and the opportunities it can present—motivation for me to attend law school at night and earn my juris doctor degree.

Of all the rote knowledge that has been placed in front of you here, if you leave with the ability to think, to understand, and the courage to take risks, then you will truly change the world. Do not ignore the common things, the day-to-day activities upon which we build our lives. It is these small changes, these little differences, that add up to make the changes that reorder society and create new orders.

There is a time for quirks and personality later. Let people know up front that you are a person of substance, not just style.

Most important to me has been his last statement: *Own it.*
I always did, and I always will.

> Do the one thing you think you cannot do.
> Fail at it. Try again. Do better the second time.
> The only people who never tumble are those who
> never mount the high wire. This is your moment.
> *Own it.* (Oprah Winfrey)

I could not avoid thinking of a great proverb that King Solomon, the wise old sage, gave to us thousands of years ago. It is found with the book of Proverbs 3:5–6:

Trust in the Lord with all of your heart and lean not only on your own understanding. In all thy ways acknowledge Him, and He shall direct thy paths.

Here is some practical advice on this new journey as a leader.

Ken Burns, the documentary filmmaker, once offered these thoughts of wisdom in a commencement speech worth repeating here:

- As you pursue your goals in life, that is to say your future, pursue your past. Let it be your guide. Insist on having a past, and then you will have a future.
- Insist on heroes. And be one.
- Read. The book is still the greatest man-made machine of all—not the car, not the TV, not the computer.
- Write. Write letters. Keep journals. Besides your children, there is no surer way of achieving immortality.
- Do not lose your enthusiasm.

Generally, the education you have received should have given you one gift in particular: the ability for critical thought.

Do not ignore the common things, the day-to-day activities upon which we build our lives.

It is these small changes, these little differences, that add up to make the changes that reorder society and create new orders.

And never believe that doing everyday tasks properly doesn't matter. George Washington Carver summed it up best when he said,

When you can do the common things of life in an uncommon way, you will command the attention of the world.

I recently heard a wonderful story from one of my former colleagues and a wonderful friend, Mark Colson, about his great-grandmother, who literally was born into European nobility.

Through the ravages of war and other man-made tragedy, she found herself in America with absolutely nothing, but not for long. She worked and saved and married and raised a wonderful, thriving family. During one of their family gatherings, one of her great-grand-children asked her what it was like to lose everything.

"I didn't lose everything," she told her gathered family. "Regardless of what man may have taken from me, the two things that sustained me and made our family strong today, they could never have taken away. Without them, I, nor any of you, would be here today. *You can never take away a person's faith or education.*"

In your leadership journey, you have had faith to surround yourself by others who have shared your convictions and beliefs and work ethic and all the other tenants that are the outward manifestation of faith.

The education that you have consumed while here will serve you for a lifetime. Hopefully, you will continue to consume all the education you can, whether in a formal, graduate, and postgraduate setting, or simply by absorbing all the knowledge that is to be had from the written and spoken word and surround yourself with people smarter than yourself.

Aristotle once said, "We are what we continually do. Excellence, therefore, is not an act, but a habit."

Knowledge, it is said, helps you make a living. Wisdom however helps you make a life.

Apply your wisdom to the world you will lead—a world you enter filled with your faith and your educational foundation to continue to learn as you lead.

Jon Meacham, who wrote the insightful biography *Destiny and Power* about our forty-first president, paints a portrait of a great leader. In his eulogy, Meacham called President Bush an *American original*.

He went on to say George H. W. Bush had a simple life code: "Tell the truth, don't blame people, be strong, do your best, try hard, forgive, stay the course. And that was—and is—the most American of creeds." That was Forty-One in a nutshell. A true leader is driven by *destiny* and by *duty*.

People often ask me about my time in the White House. When did you first meet President Bush, and were you first a part of his governmental or political operation?

So it began in 1985 when I was retained as a political consultant to the Fund for America's Future. The two leaders of that federal political action committee were Lee Atwater, who would ultimately head the presidential election campaign for then-vice president Bush and become Republican National Committee chairman in 1989, and Rich Bond, who was Vice President Bush's deputy chief of staff and, in 1991, became the chairman of the Republican National Committee where I would serve as his chief of staff.

My first national political assignment was to travel to Michigan in 1986 to participate in the write-in for precinct delegates scheduled for August. I moved into Lansing, Michigan, in June and stayed until mid-August. Michigan would become the first major battle of the 1988 Republican primary for president while putting our campaign on the ground in what others described as political hand-to-hand combat with both the Pat Robertson and Jack Kemp presidential campaigns while Bob Dole sidestepped the entire process.

We won as Bush came out on top with more than 50 percent of the delegates elected in the three-man field. My involvement in Michigan in the summer of 1986 was captured in the book *Whose Broad Stripes and Bright Stars* by legendary political journalists Jack Germond and Jules Witcover.

We declared victory in Michigan, and I moved on.

My next assignment would place me in both the Hawaii Caucus (December 1987) and the Maine Caucus (January 1988) as a political troubleshooter, and I was later assigned to the Republican National Convention in New Orleans that summer.

After the November election, I was appointed the director of all first-family operations at the inauguration and became a White House staff appointee as a special assistant to the president of the United States.

When I reported for duty on my first day of work in the White House in February 1989, I was met by a person who would, over the years, become my best friend and brother, Sichan Siv. He walked into my office and handed me the *marching orders* from the president:

- Think big.
- Challenge the system.
- Adhere to the highest ethical standards.
- Be on the record as much as possible.
- Fight hard for your position.
- When I make a call, we move as a team.
- Represent the United States of America with dignity.

Sichan is a unique and remarkable individual.

Born and educated in Cambodia, he was the son of a police chief and loving mother but would learn years later that he was the only surviving member of his family of seven. In 1975, he found himself working as an employee of the United States relief agency who became a target for the Khmer Rouge, which rose to power when Pol Pot overthrew the government.

The Khmer Rouge began a vicious genocide imprisoning, enslaving, and murdering the educated members of the Cambodian society the same year the United States withdraw from Vietnam. The "killing fields" would mark the period of time when the Khmer Rouge soldiers killed 1.7 million Cambodians. Fearing for his life, Sichan set out on a bicycle seeking safety, only to find himself being captured and put in a slave camp.

Knowing he was marked for execution, Sichan made a daring escape by jumping off the rear of a moving logging truck and running for freedom into Thailand. He was placed in a refugee camp for months before coming to America. In 2008, he published his best-selling book about his life: *Golden Bones*.

During our time together in the White House, Sichan would often invite me to his office to meet some very interesting people who he would be responsible for escorting into the Oval Office for presidential meetings. Some included Eric Clapton, Michael Jackson, Miss America, Miss Universe, Joe DiMaggio, and Ted Williams. On one occasion, he asked me to meet him in the Rose Garden because he was escorting an individual to the president's upstairs residence. That was the day I was introduced to the Dalai Lama. Sichan taught me that leadership matters by being a living example of courage, hope, and faith. He and his wife Martha would become special people in my life.

In 2001, President George W. Bush would nominate Sichan to become an ambassador to the United Nations, and he was unanimously confirmed by the US Senate. When I celebrate the Fourth of July, my thoughts always turn to Sichan and his life journey.

Serving under President George H. W. Bush was a great privilege and a true lesson in observing what a leader is while demonstrating a belief of having more faith in us that we had in ourselves.

A popular quote I've heard from others is "The best leadership tool you have is your example." The forty-first president led us all by these examples:

- Leaders need to change, to keep reinventing themselves.
- Leaders have to be ready to adept to move, to forget yesterday, to forgive, and to structure new roles and new relationships for themselves, their teams, and their ever-shifting portfolio of partners.

Questions to Ponder on Your Leadership Journey

- Are you decisive?
- Are you readily approachable?
- Is your attitude positive and proactive?
- Do you delegate without exception?
- Do you do what you expect others to do?

Simple Leadership Lessons for Others to Follow You

- Surround yourself with individuals who take their work seriously but not themselves—those who work hard and play hard.
- You need to have both strong ideas and be an optimist. Embrace being a problem-solver and relentless preparation.
- Inject just enough humor on *all* occasions to make life manageable while displaying courage when dealing with fear.

I always loved my work.

During my fifteen-plus years as the leader of the Business Council of Alabama, I had a simple leadership philosophy: "I tried not to take ourselves too seriously. We enjoyed fighting for what we believed in. We enjoyed fighting back. We loved finding allies. And—famously—we enjoyed making enemies, as a last resort! And in the end, we tried not to make any permanent enemies over any single issue or argument."

Leadership is all about inspiring others with healthy doses of empathy, humility, and grace to empower those that follow.

The one constant in the workplace is the human element. Despite all the technological advances, people still are just people.

The performance level of individuals is often measured largely through ability, likability, and drive.

Leadership, by contrast, demands a broader range of character traits, including high levels of integrity and low levels of behaviors born out of negative attributes. Great leaders however are able to remain open and to adapt no matter how experienced they are. They succeed because they are able to continually learn.

And encourage yourself to think ahead of the box.

People want to be respected and allowed to do meaningful work, to be recognized and rewarded for the work they do, and to feel they are part of something bigger—some vision or mission. Those qualities are timeless, so articulating your understanding of that will demonstrate that you are a leader for all seasons.

This will define you as a leader: never be discouraged and never hold back give everything you got. Be open to people and ideas.

And when you fail throughout your life, remember this: fall forward and repeat these six simple words from William Borden, as you begin again *No reserves. No retreats. No regrets.*

ACKNOWLEDGMENTS

This is the place in the book where I attempt to thank those who influenced and impacted my life, career, work, direction, and my faith and so many who became mentors along the journey.

It is impossible to do that. I would need to list hundreds and hundreds of people.

That, in its own right, is a blessing.

I will thank by name my beautiful, amazing, and loving wife and my rock Leura, along with my loving children Margaret and Will, who always make me proud. You inspire me. You support me. You believe in me, and you love me. I have been blessed beyond what I deserve. Leura deserves to know how much I appreciated her support, love, friendship on joining me as my copilot on this journey.

My brother Gordon Canary, along with my sisters Charlene Stockton and Christina Bouffard, always providing love, encouragement, unwavering support, and having faith in all that I do. My loving mother Trudy and my dad Bill Canary—they established the foundation for what would become the rest of my life. I only wish they were still here. They were my "always people"—always there and always able to provide love, support, hope, and inspiration while believing in me unconditionally.

Susan and Dorman Walker whose friendship, support, and love have inspired our entire family in ways that are immeasurable.

My governmental and political career would not have occurred without the inspiration of Mayor Gil Hanse; Mayor Don Conroy; Mayor Ralph Scordino (Babylon Village, New York); the forty-first president of the United States, George H. W. Bush; Congressman

Robert Aderholt; Brian Rell; Governor Bob Riley; Mary Matalin; Rich Bond; former Alabama Speaker of the House Mike Hubbard; Congressman Mike Rogers; Karl Rove; Mayor Sandy Stimpson; Bubba Lee; Debra Anderson; Caroline Aderholt; Walter White; Scott Reed; Andy Card; Jo Bonner; Tony Noto; Bill Ellis; Mike Dawidziak; Bill Dal Col; Ray Allmendinger; Ambassador Sichan Siv; Jimmy McLaughlin, Paul Aniboli and Will Sellers.

Thank you to the hundreds of colleagues who made the impossible look easy when I served as president and CEO of both the American Trucking Associations (ATA), the Business Council of Alabama (BCA).

The Chamber Association of Commerce of Alabama (CCAA), Tom Donohue, Jay Timmons, Leslie Hortum, Suzanne Clark, Frank Filgo, Rob Engstrom, Duane Acklie, Steve Brooks, Michael Lowry, Charles Nailen, Perry Hand, Tommy Lee, Carl Jamison, Will Brooke, Sandy Stimpson, Jeff Coleman, Carol Gordy, Johnny Johns, Marty Abroms, Mark Colson, Mark Wilson, John Milne, Susan Carothers, Nathan Lindsay, Dave Steward, Ted Hosp, John Seymour, Donna Watts, Rick Roden, Jim Page, Jeremy Arthur, David Azbell, Chris Clark, Joe Watkins, Doug Loon, Glenn Hamer, Sara Armstrong, Raymond Towle, Dr. Joe Morton, Jay Love and John Anzalone for always having my back and always giving unconditional support.

My walk of faith was impacted by Dr. Karl Stegall, Father Kuzma, Father Mulligan, Sister Maureen Peters, Ambassador Sichan Siv, Dr. Sandy Benkwith and Charles Nailen.

My world-class medical team led by Dr. John Fiveash, Dr. Mollie Deshazo, and Dr. Rakesh Patel, who always gave me 100 percent all the time while being painfully honest.

I am forever indebted to David Azbell, who has spent countless hours to help me edit this book and direct my thinking on how best to organize my writing. David is a gifted writer, and I can't thank him enough for being my friend.

Thank you seems inadequate to everyone in my life.

NOTES

Author's Note
- http://goodreads.com/quotes/andy_andrews
- *Inaugural Address*: President George H.W. Bush, January 20, 1989.
- Barry Black Seventh-day Adventist Senate Chaplain: *Prayer to the joint session of Congress*, January 7, 2021.

Introduction
- http://goodreads.com/quotes/john_quincy_adams
- http://goodreads.com/quotes/john_wesley
- http://goodreads.com/quotes/mary_oliver.
- *"Getting Off on The Right Foot:"* The Prophet, February 13, 1968
- *http://outreachmagazine.com/features/discipleship/*quotes/william_borden

Chapter 1
- http://goodreads.com/quotes/ronald_reagan

Chapter 2
- http://goodreads.com'quotes/john_maxwell
- Andrews, Andy. *The Butterfly Effect,* Nashville: Thomas Nelson, 2010
- Taylor, Paige. Handwritten Note, 2019
- Photo Credits: Josh Vaughn, Business Council of Alabama

Chapter 3
- www.executivespeak.com/2015/02/10/top-10-quotes-on -communication-skills-and-leadership/gilbert_amelio
- http://www/brainyquote.com/quotes/mahatma_gandhi
- Courtesy: Reagan Presidential Library/President Reagan's Humor from Selected Stories, 1981-1989/Diaper Story

Chapter 4:
- *"Canary Offers No Apology for the Industry:"* Transport Topics, October 28, 2002
- Editorial: *"Passing the Baton:"* Transport Topics, January 16, 2003
- http://www/brianyquote.com/quotes/alan_alda

Chapter 5:
- www.advice.theshineapp.com/quotes/yoda
- www.teaandtheology.com/: Good Tired-A Reflection on Harry Chapin's Quote
- *Choosing Alabama's next State Superintendent:* William J. Canary and Joe Morton Alabama Voices Montgomery Advertiser, July 15, 2016 and Education Graphic by Anatoliy Babiy/Getty Images/iStock Photo/Licensed to William Canary File ID:468209151)

Chapter 6
- http://www/brainyquote.com/quotes/michael_jordan
- http://goodreads.com/quotes/richard_branson
- http://goodreads.com/quotes/winston_churchill
- http://goodreads.com/quotes/tony_robbin

Chapter 7
- Governor Kay Ivey, *State of the State Address*, March 5, 2019
- *Early Childcare Has $1 billion Economic Impact and Long-Lasting Business Benefits:* Dana Beyerle, BEA Report and Business Council of Alabama publication, December 16, 2013
- http://goodreads.com/quotes/albert_einstein

Chapter 8
- http://goodreads.com/quotes/bob_proctor
- Smith, Judy. *Good Self, Bad Self: How to Bounce Back from a Personal Crisis*: New York: Free Press, 2013
- Hand, Perry, Chairman Business Council of Alabama, *Statement*, April 12, 2018
- http://goodreads.com/quotes/winston_churchill
- Canary, William, *Statement* Executive Committee, Business Council of Alabama, April 10, 2018
- Canary, William, (Author) Business Council of Alabama: *The Plan-Transition and Succession*, May 21, 2018
- Hand, Perry, Chairman Business Council of Alabama, *Report to Leadership,* June 8, 2018
- Press Release: *BCA's Canary Announces Departure, Accepts Position at US Chamber*, July 6, 2018
- Smith, Judy. *Good Self, Bad Self: How to Bounce Back from a Personal Crisis*: New York: Free Press, 2013
- http://goodreads.com/quotes/colin_powell

Chapter 9
- http://www/brainyquote.com/quotes/davidben_gurion
- http//www/mdanderson.org/*Why do cancer patients ring the bell after treatment?* October 28, 1019

Epilogue: Own It
- http://goodreads.com/quotes/john_wooden
- http://goodreads.com/quotes/vincentvan_gogh
- http://www/brainyquote.com/quotes/oprah_winfrey
- http:/www/biblegate.com/Proverbs 3:5-6 NIV
- Burns, Ken, *Commencement Address at Georgetown University*, 2006
- http://www.townandcountrymag.com: John Meacham's Eulogy for George H.W. Bush, December 5, 2018
- *Marching Orders from the President of the United States to Staff,* January 20,1989

ABOUT THE AUTHOR

With more than forty years of experience in leadership and public service at the national level, William "Billy" Canary has devoted his career to building and growing organizations and pushing them to succeed. Canary began his professional career in New York, where he made an early name for himself in the political arena, winning several elected positions in the Long Island area. His success caught the eye of leaders within the Republican Party and soon led to key appointments as special assistant to President George H. W. Bush and as chief of staff at the Republican National Committee.

Since leaving the White House, he has become a tireless advocate for businesses and a champion of economic growth, holding roles as CEO of the American Trucking Associations and the Business Council of Alabama.

While at BCA, Canary served as an advisor to Alabama governor Bob Riley and helped conceive, develop, and promote some of the nation's most innovative and award-winning K-12 education programs. Canary was previously a senior fellow for the United States Chamber of Commerce and is a faculty member for the Chamber Foundation's Institute for Organization Management.

He currently operates Canary & Company Consulting, which utilizes his strong knowledge of business, economics, leadership skills, and politics to help chamber executives and association leaders solve complex challenges. Canary is a contributor and coauthor of *The Next New Start* (2015), *Unfinished Business* (2016), *Time And Again* (2017), and the author of *Leadership: No Reserves. No Retreats. No Regrets* (2021).

A graduate of State University New York at Oneonta, Canary holds a Juris Doctor from the Jacob D. Fuchsberg Law Center at Touro College. He and his wife Leura have two grown children, Will and Margaret; and he splits his time between Montgomery, Alabama, and Miramar Beach, Florida.

CPSIA information can be obtained
at www.ICGtesting.com
Printed in the USA
BVHW030254190123
656443BV00028B/217